W9-BRF-006

Crochet in No Time

Crochet
in No Time

A Simple, Stylish Collection
of **52** Quick-Crochet Projects

Melody Griffiths

Reader's
Digest

The Reader's Digest Association, Inc.
Pleasantville, New York / Montreal

A READER'S DIGEST BOOK

This edition published by The Reader's Digest Association, Inc., by arrangement with
CICO BOOKS
an imprint of Ryland Peters & Small Ltd
20-21 Jockeys Fields
London
WC1R 4BW

FOR CICO BOOKS
Editor: Marie Clayton
Designer: Roger Hammond
Photographer: Tino Tedaldi

FOR READER'S DIGEST
U.S. Project Editor: Barbara Booth
Consulting Editor: Jane Townswick
Canadian Project Editor: Pamela Johnson
Project Designer: Mabel Zorzano
Associate Art Director: George McKeon
Executive Editor, Trade Publishing: Dolores York
Associate Publisher: Rosanne McManus
President and Publisher, Trade Publishing: Harold Clarke

Library of Congress Cataloging-in-Publication Data

Griffiths, Melody.
    Crochet in no time : A Simple, Stylish Collection of 52 Quick-Crochet Projects / Melody Griffiths.
      p. cm.
    ISBN-13: 978-0-7621-0817-6
    ISBN-10: 0-7621-0817-7
    1. Crocheting–Patterns. 2. Clothing and dress. 3. Dress accessories–Patterns. I. Title.

TT825.G6836 2007
746,43'7041–dc22
                              2006052236

Address any comments about *Crochet in No Time* to:
    The Reader's Digest Association, Inc.
    Adult Trade Publishing
    Reader's Digest Road
    Pleasantville, NY 10570-7000

For more Reader's Digest products and information, visit our website:
    www.rd.com (in the United States)
    www.readersdigest.ca (in Canada)
    www.rdasia.com (in Asia)

Printed in China

1 3 5 7 9 10 8 6 4 2

Note to Our Readers
The editors who produced this book have attempted to make the contents as accurate and correct as possible. Illustrations, photographs, and text have been carefully checked. All instructions should be reviewed and understood by the reader before undertaking any project. The directions and designs for the projects in this publication are under copyright. These projects may be reproduced for the reader's personal use or for gifts. Reproduction for sale or profit is forbidden by law.

Contents

Introduction

Crochet is so simple and so versatile. All you need to get started is a hook and some yarn. The action of catching and looping the yarn soon builds up into stitches, making crochet one of the fastest ways of creating a fabric. And the feel of the fabric can vary enormously, depending on the combination of hook size, yarn type, and stitch pattern; crochet can be firm, floppy, lacy, textured, soft, crisp, flat, or three-dimensional.

My mother taught me to crochet when I was about five years old. I can still remember how easy it was to make the stitches and how exciting it was to see the work grow. But it's only been in the last few years that I've extended my knowledge and experience as a hand-knit designer to creating garments using those basic crochet stitches learned so long ago.

This book is about crochet in a modern context. With a stunning collection of more than 50 things to make, you have the choice of creating items for your home, for yourself, or for family and friends.

With these designs, I've tried to find new ways of exploring and exploiting simple crochet stitches and techniques. Sometimes this means breaking the rules and substituting a single crochet and two chain for the more usual three turning chain to give a neater edge, or choosing a fancy fashion yarn rather than the classic smooth yarns usually associated with crochet. And wherever possible, I've tried to make the stitch patterns simpler to do—for instance, working into spaces rather than into chain to make it easier to see where to place the hook for fine lacework or when working with heavily textured yarns.

If you've never tried crochet before, the techniques section will provide you with everything you need to know to get started. And the nicest thing about crochet is that once you've grasped the basics, you can make anything. Each project indicates the time it takes to crochet the item, as well as tips to help you decide if a project is right for you and your lifestyle.

There are projects worked in the round, projects worked in rows, projects that took less than an hour to make, scrap-yarn projects, heirloom projects, projects for beginners, and projects that require more determination. There are unusual motifs and original ideas—everything from simple scarves and wraps to toys, shapely garments, lacy trims, and heirloom baby clothes. With so many to choose from, you're sure to find some that are irresistible.

Happy crocheting!

Melody

Scarves, Wraps, Hats & Gloves

Simple Shell Scarf

This versatile design shows what a difference the yarn makes. Whether you create a country effect or choose a more sophisticated style, all you need to know for the one-row pattern used for this beautiful scarf is how to do chain and double crochet. The pretty stitch has rows of shells with spaces between, so it's easy to see exactly where you are in the pattern, and because each row measures almost an inch, it grows quickly too.

ESTIMATED TIME TO COMPLETE

Each row of shell pattern took about 3 minutes. Total time taken for the shorter scarf 4 hours; for the longer scarf 6 hours.

ABOUT THESE YARNS

Debbie Bliss Soho is a 100 percent pure wool hand-spun yarn that's dyed to give a rich multicolor effect. It has 70 yd. (65 m) to a 50-g ball. Debbie Bliss Cashmerino Aran is a mix of 55 percent merino wool, 33 percent microfiber, and 12 percent cashmere. It has 98 yd. (90 m) to a 50-g ball.

SIZES

Multicolor scarf width 6¼ in. (16 cm); **length** 51 in. (130 cm); **pink scarf width** 5½ in. (14 cm); **length** 79 in. (200 cm)

YOU WILL NEED

FOR THE MULTICOLOR SCARF

■ 4 x 50-g balls of Debbie Bliss Soho in shade 09
■ E/4 (3.50-mm) crochet hook

FOR THE PINK SCARF

■ 5 x 50-g balls of Debbie Bliss Cashmerino Aran in shade 616
■ H/8 (5.00-mm) crochet hook

GAUGE

multicolor scarf: Four shell patts measure 6⅜ in. (16 cm), 6 rows to 4 in. (10 cm) over shell patt using E/4 (3.50-mm) hook. **pink scarf:** Four shell patts measure 5½ in. (14 cm), 7 rows to 4 in. (10 cm) over shell patt using H/8 (5.00-mm) hook. Change hook size if necessary to obtain these gauges.

ABBREVIATIONS

ch = chain; **dc** = double crochet; **patt(s)** = pattern(s); **[ ]** = work instructions in brackets as directed.

TIPS

■ The scarf is worked in two halves from the center so that the shell pattern will run in the same direction on both sides when the ends of the scarf hang down.

■ Make the starting chain loosely; if necessary, use a larger size hook.

■ There is no right or wrong side to the pattern, which makes the scarf fully reversible.

■ Each half of the scarf in Soho takes two balls of yarn, so you can keep working until you run out. If you want to count the rows, there should be 39 rows in each half.

■ The scarf in Cashmerino Aran takes just over two balls for each half, so you could make it longer if you prefer. If you want to count the rows, there should be 70 rows in each half.

■ If you prefer a wider scarf, add six chains for each extra shell and repeat the instructions in square brackets one more time for each extra shell. If you make the scarf wider, remember to buy extra yarn or your scarf won't be as long as in the pictures.

SCARF

First half Make 27ch.

Row 1 5dc in 6th ch from hook, [skip 2ch, 1dc in next ch, skip 2ch, 5dc in next ch] 3 times, skip 2ch, 1dc in last ch.

Row 2 3ch, skip first dc, [skip next 2dc, 5dc in next dc, skip next 2dc, 1dc in next dc] 4 times, working last dc in top ch.

The 2nd row forms the shell patt.

For the multicolor scarf Work until the scarf measures 25½ in. (65 cm) from starting chain. Fasten off.

For the pink scarf Work until the scarf measures 39½ in. (100 cm) from starting chain. Fasten off.

Both scarves. Second half Join yarn in first ch of first row. Working into chain on first row, complete as first half. Fasten off. Darn in ends.

Choose richly colored hand-spun wool or a mix of smooth, vibrant cashmere yarn to make this easy scarf.

Pansy-Motif Scarf

This pretty scarf is a scrap-yarn project. The naturalistic effect of the pansy motif is enhanced by working it in shades of purple and pink with a flash of yellow at the center. Different height stitches make lifelike petals, with chain gaps in the last round to flute the edges and give a convenient place to join the motifs. The rows of pansies are sewn on a simple mesh scarf that's really quick to work.

ESTIMATED TIME TO COMPLETE
Each pansy took 20 minutes; complete scarf 9 hours.

ABOUT THIS YARN
The yarn used for the pansies and the scarf is a smooth, pure wool sport-weight yarn with approximately 120 yd. (110 m) to a 50-g ball.

SIZE
Width 6¼ in. (16 cm); **length** 48 in. (122 cm)

YOU WILL NEED
For the pansies
■ 1 x 50-g ball in shades of yellow (A), 1 x 50-g ball in black, wine, or eggplant (B), and 1 x 50-g ball in lilac, purple, or pink (C), all in pure wool sport-weight yarn
For the scarf
■ 70 g pure wool sport-weight yarn in soft green (D)
For both
■ E/4 (3.50-mm) crochet hook

GAUGE
Each pansy motif measures 2½ in. (6.5 cm) wide and 2¾ in. (7 cm) high, 5 spaces and 8 rows to 4 in. (10 cm) over mesh patt, when pressed, using E/4 (3.50-mm) hook. Change hook size if necessary to obtain this size motif and this gauge.

ABBREVIATIONS
ch = chain; **cont** = continue; **dc** = double crochet; **dtr** = double triple; **hdc** = half-double crochet; **RS** = right side; **sc** = single crochet; **sp(s)** = spaces; **ss** = slip stitch; **tr** = triple; **WS** = wrong side; **[ ]** = work instructions in brackets as directed.

TIPS
■ Yarn amounts are approximate and may vary according to the brand and fiber content of the sport-weight yarn you use.
■ To work the long sc stitches. insert the hook in 2ch sp of first round as directed and pull the loop up to the height of the 4th round, tension the strands to lie flat on the motif between the two dc stitches of the 2nd round, then complete the dc.
■ Changing the colors you use for A, B, and C adds to the flowery effect.
■ Finish your motifs quickly and neatly by working over the ends and snipping them off; then you'll only need to darn in the last end.
■ Different brands of sport-weight yarn may be slightly different in thickness, so the size of the pansy motifs could vary slightly.
■ If you prefer, instead of joining the pansies in rows, just scatter them at random all over the scarf.

PANSY MOTIF
Using A, make 4ch, ss in first ch to form a ring. Cont in A.
Round 1 (RS) 1ch, [1sc, 2ch] 6 times in ring, ss in first sc. Fasten off.
Join B in a 2ch sp.

Round 2 (RS) 1ch, 1sc in same sp as join, [2ch, 2sc in next sp] 5 times, 2ch, 1sc in first sp, ss in first sc.

Round 3 Ss in next sp, [1ch, 1hdc, ss] in same sp as first ss, [ss, 3ch, 4dc, 3ch, ss] in each of next 2 sps, [ss, 1hdc, ss] in foll sp, [ss, 1ch, 3sc, 1ch, ss] in each of next 2 sps, ss in first sp. Fasten off.

Join C to the right of the first large petal.

Round 4 1ch, inserting hook in 2ch sp of first round below, work 1 long sc, continue working behind petals made on 2nd and 3rd rounds, [5ch, 1 long sc in next sp of first round] twice, 3ch, [1 long sc in next sp of first round, 4ch] twice, 1 long sc in last sp of first round, 3ch, ss in first sc.

Round 5 [1sc, 1hdc, 1dc, 1ch, 1dc, 3tr, 1ch, 3tr, 1dc, 1ch, 1dc, 1hdc, 1sc] in each 5ch sp, [1sc, 1dc, 1ch, 1dc, ss] in 3ch sp, [ss, 1hdc, 1dc, 1ch, 3dc, 1ch, 1dc, 1hdc, ss] in each 4ch sp, [ss, 1dc, 1ch, 1dc, 1sc] in 3ch sp, ss in first sc. Fasten off.

Make 18 motifs, joining in rows of 3 by working 1sc instead of 1ch in corresponding 1ch sp of large and small petals.

SCARF

First side Using D, make 34ch.

Row 1 (RS) 1sc in 2nd ch from hook, [6ch, skip 3ch, 1sc in next ch] 8 times.

Row 2 8ch, 1sc in first 6ch sp, [6ch, 1sc in next 6ch sp] 7 times, 3ch, 1dtr in last sc.

Row 3 1sc in dtr, [6ch, 1sc in next 6ch sp] 7 times, 6ch, 1sc in 5th ch.

Rows 2 and 3 form the mesh pattern. Work 43 more rows. Fasten off.

2nd side Work as first side, do not fasten off.

Joining row With WS together and 2nd side facing, work 1sc in 5th ch of first side, [4ch, 1sc in next 6ch sp of both sides together] 7 times, 4ch, 1sc in 5th ch of 2nd side and dtr of first side together. Fasten off. Darn in ends.

TO FINISH

Press scarf to open out the mesh. With short ends of scarf level with center of first row of pansies, sew three rows of three pansies on each end of the scarf.

These pretty pansies grow very quickly and bloom all year long.

Scarf with Pockets

Superchunky yarn and simple stitches on a huge hook make this a quick-to-finish project. Tuck your hands into the patch pockets or use them to hold small items.

ESTIMATED TIME TO COMPLETE

The scarf took 2 hours.

ABOUT THIS YARN

Rowan Big Wool is a very thick yarn with two soft strands lightly twisted together. It's 100 percent merino wool with approximately 87 yd. (80 m) to a 100-g ball.

SIZE

Width 8¼ in. (21 cm); **length** 65½ in. (166.5 cm)

YOU WILL NEED

■ 3 x 100-g balls of Rowan Big Wool in Pistachio, shade 029 (A)

■ 1 x 100-g ball same in Whoosh, shade 014 (B)

■ P/16 (12.00-mm) crochet hook

GAUGE

6 sts and 8 rows to 4 in. (10 cm) over single crochet using P/16 (12.00-mm) hook. Change hook size if necessary to obtain this gauge.

ABBREVIATIONS

ch = chain; **cont** = continue; **RS** = right side; **sc** = single crochet; **st(s)** = stitch(es); **WS** = wrong side; **[ ]** = work instructions in brackets as directed.

TIPS

■ Work the starting chain very loosely. Each chain loop should be almost ⅞ in. (2 cm) long.

■ When working the last row of sc, tension the loop at the top of each stitch to match the starting chain.

■ The pockets in the picture are left open at the top. If you prefer, you could leave them open at the sides.

■ For an even quicker and simpler scarf, simply leave off the pockets.

SCARF

Using A, make 101ch.

Row 1 (WS) Working into back loop each time, 1sc in 2nd ch from hook, [1sc in each ch] to end. 100 sts.

Row 2 1ch, [1sc in each sc] to end. The 2nd row forms single crochet. Cont in sc, work 15 more rows. Fasten off.

Pockets (Make 2) Using B, make 9ch. Work first row as given for scarf. 8 sts. Work 9 rows sc. Fasten off. Darn in ends.

TO FINISH

Press according to ball band. Pin pockets in place on RS at each end of scarf. Using A, work surface chain around three sides of each pocket. Sew pocket edges under surface chain and remove pins.

Keep your hands
warm, too, when you
wrap up in this cozy
multipurpose scarf.

Shaded Fluted Scarf

Increasing along one edge makes a deep ruffle that automatically curls around to give a soft fluted effect. The scarf is worked in double crochet on a chain and single crochet base.

ESTIMATED TIME TO COMPLETE
The scarf took 6½ hours.

ABOUT THIS YARN
Rowan Kid Silk Haze is an ultra-fine yarn that's a mix of 70 percent super-kid mohair and 30 percent silk. It has approximately 229 yd. (210 m) to a 25-g ball.

SIZE
Width 3½ in. (8 cm); **length** (along shorter edge) 56¼ in. (143 cm)

YOU WILL NEED
■ 1 x 25-g ball of Rowan Kid Silk Haze in each of Liqueur, shade 595 (A); Candy Girl, shade 606 (B); and Grace, shade 580 (C)
■ I/9 (5.50-mm) crochet hook

GAUGE
13 sts in single crochet and 6 rows in patt to 3⅛ in. (8 cm) using I/9 (5.50-mm) hook. Change hook size if necessary to obtain this gauge.

ABBREVIATIONS
ch = chain; **dc** = double; **foll** = following; **patt** = pattern; **sc** = single crochet; **st(s)** = stitch(es); **[ ]** = work instructions in brackets as directed.

NOTE
The hook size given is larger than would usually be used with this yarn to give a very soft, open fabric.

TIP
If you want to make the scarf all in one color, you'll need just two balls of Rowan Kid Silk Haze yarn.

SCARF
Using A, make 198ch.
Row 1 1sc in 2nd ch from hook, [1sc in each ch] to end. 197 sts.
Row 2 1sc in first sc, 2ch, [1dc in each sc] to end.
Row 3 1sc in first dc, 2ch, [2dc in next dc, 1dc in foll dc] to last 2 sts, 2dc in next dc, 1dc in 2nd ch. 295 sts.
Change to B.
Row 4 1sc in first dc, 2ch, [2dc in each of next 2dc, 1dc in foll dc] to last 3 sts, 2dc in each of next 2dc, 1dc in 2nd ch. 491 sts.
Row 5 1sc in first dc, 2ch, [2dc in each of next 4dc, 1dc in foll dc] to end, placing last dc in 2nd ch. 883 sts.
Change to C.
Row 6 1sc in first dc, [1dc in next dc, 2dc in each of next 6dc, 1dc in each of foll 2dc] to end, placing last dc in 2nd ch. 1471 sts.
Fasten off. Darn in ends.

Get two looks from this fine mohair-and-silk scarf; let the edges flute

for a soft ruffle effect, or let it twist for a pretty rope of bell shapes.

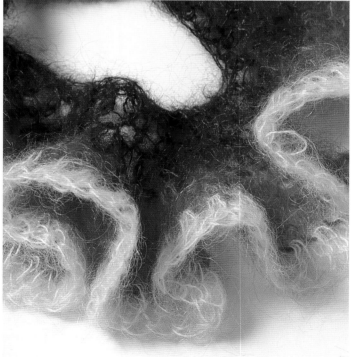

Black Lace Wrap

Despite its sophisticated appearance, this wrap is quick and easy to make. The motifs are open and lacy, with most of the groups of stitches that make up the pattern worked into chain spaces, which makes them easy to see and do. The beads that enhance the design are sewn on afterward, so you can add as many or as few as you want.

ESTIMATED TIME TO COMPLETE
Each motif takes 40 minutes; finished wrap 6 hours.

ABOUT THIS YARN
Rowan Lurex Shimmer is a lightweight metallic yarn. It is a mix of 80 percent viscose and 20 percent polyester with approximately 104 yd. (95 m) to a 25-g ball.

SIZE
Width 16 in. (41 cm); **length** 57½ in. (146 cm).

YOU WILL NEED
■ 5 x 25-g balls of Rowan Lurex Shimmer in black, shade 334
■ No. 6 steel (1.75-mm) crochet hook
■ assorted beads and sequins
■ black sewing thread and sharp needle

GAUGE
Each 10-round motif measures 8¼ in. (21 cm) across; edging measures 4 in. (10 cm), all when pressed, using No. 6 steel (1.75-mm) hook. Change hook size if necessary to obtain this size motif.

ABBREVIATIONS
ch = chain; **dc** = double; **dtr** = double triple; **rep** = repeat; **RS** = right side; **sc** = single crochet; **sp(s)** = space(s); **ss** = slip stitch; **st(s)** = stitch(es); **tr** = triple; **[ ]** = work instructions in brackets as directed.

TIPS
■ Work two motifs from each ball of yarn, then use the leftover yarn for the edging.
■ It's easier to hide the darned-in ends if you join in new yarn while working a double or double triple group.
■ You don't have to add beads; the wrap works well without.
■ The wrap in the picture mixes teardrop shapes and different sizes of round silver, pink, and purple metallic beads with pink and green cupped sequins, but you could use any combination of beads and sequins.
■ Choose just gold- or silver-colored beads for a wrap to match any outfit.

MOTIF
Make 8ch, ss in first ch to form a ring.
Round 1 (RS) 7ch, [1tr in ring, 3ch] 10 times, 1tr in ring, 1dc in 4th ch. 12 sps.
Round 2 1ch, 1sc in first sp, [5ch, 1sc in next sp] 11 times, 2ch, 1dc in first sc.
Round 3 1sc in first sp, 2ch, 2dc in same sp, [5ch, 3dc in next sp] 11 times, 2ch, 1dc in 2nd ch.

Round 4 1ch, 1sc in first sp, [7ch, 1sc in next sp] 11 times, 1ch, 1tr in first sc.
Round 5 1sc in first sp, 2ch, 2dc in first sp, [7ch, 3dc in next sp] 11 times, 3ch, 1tr in 2nd ch.
Round 6 1ch, 1sc in first sp, [9ch, 1sc in next sp] 11 times, 3ch, 1dtr in first sc.

Round 7 1ch, 1sc in first sp, 5ch, 1sc in same sp, * [5ch, 1sc] twice in next sp, rep from * to last sp, 1sc in first sp, 2ch, 1dc in first sc.
Round 8 As Round 4, but working instructions in square brackets 23 times.
Round 9 As Round 3, but working instructions in square brackets 23 times.
Round 10 As Round 6, but working instructions in square brackets 23 times. Fasten off.

JOIN MOTIFS

Work 2nd motif in same way as first motif until Round 9 has been completed.

Round 10 1ch, 1sc in first sp, [9ch, 1sc in next sp] 20 times, [4ch, 1sc in corresponding sp of first motif, 4ch, 1sc in next sp of 2nd motif] 3 times, 4ch 1sc in last sp of first motif, 4ch, ss in first sc of 2nd motif. Make and join four more motifs in the same way to make a strip of six motifs.

EDGING

With RS facing, join yarn in sp to the right of the join between 3rd and 4th motifs.

Round 1 1ch, 1sc in same place as join, 4ch, 1sc in first sp of next motif, [9ch, 1sc in next sp] 8 times, 4ch, [1sc in next sp, 9ch] 8 times, 1sc in foll sp, 4ch, [1sc in next sp, 9ch] 20 times, * 1sc in foll sp, 4ch, [1sc in next sp, 9ch] 8 times, rep from * 3 more times, 1sc in foll sp, 4ch, [1sc in next sp, 9ch] 20 times, 1sc in foll sp, 4ch, [1sc in next sp, 9ch] 8 times, 1sc in foll sp, 4 ch, [1dc in next sp, 9ch] 7 times, 1sc in foll sp, 4ch, 1dtr in first dc.

Round 2 1ch, 1sc in same place as join, 2ch, 2dc in same place as join, 1ch, * 3dc in first sp of next motif, [9ch, 3dc in next sp] 7 times, 1ch, rep from * once more, then rep from * working instructions in square brackets 19 times, rep from * 4 times, then rep again working instructions in square brackets 19 times, rep from * once more, then rep again working instructions in square brackets 6 times, 4ch, 1dtr in 2nd ch.

Round 3 1sc in dtr sp, 2ch, 2dc in same sp, 1ch, working instructions in square brackets 6, 18 or 5 times as appropriate, complete as Round 2.

Working instructions in square brackets one less time on each repeat, work two more rounds in the same way as Round 2 and 3.

Round 6 1sc in dtr sp, 4ch, 2dtr in same sp, 7ch, [3dtr, 7ch] twice in each sp to end, 3dtr in first sp, 7ch, ss in 4th ch.

TO FINISH

Darn in ends. Press according to ball band. Sew beads and sequins on centers of motifs by slipping the needle through the crochet stitches to hide the thread after sewing on each bead or sequin. Fasten off between sewing on groups of beads and sequins around the outer edge of the wrap.

Skinny Scarf & Evening Wrap

Choose from an alluring little scarf or a gorgeous cover-up; they're both in a simple openwork stitch pattern that grows very quickly and shows off the fabulous texture of the yarn.

ESTIMATED TIME TO COMPLETE

Total time taken for the skinny scarf 45 minutes; for the wrap 4 hours.

ABOUT THIS YARN

Sirdar Vegas is a lightweight yarn with a tightly twisted, shiny core with metallic and multicolored tags and tassels, for a textured effect. It's a 75 percent polyester, 25 percent acrylic mix, with 71 yd. (65 m) to a 50-g ball.

SIZES

SCARF: **width** 2 in. (5 cm); **length** 55 in. (140 cm) WRAP: **width** 16¼ in. (41.5 cm); **length** 54¼ in. (138 cm). In the instructions, the first figure refers to the scarf; figures in parentheses refer to the wrap.

YOU WILL NEED

For the scarf

■ 1 x 50-g ball of Sirdar Vegas, in Roulette, shade 120

For the wrap

■ 5 x 50-g balls of Sirdar Vegas, in Roulette, shade 120

For both

■ I/9 (5.50-mm) crochet hook

GAUGE

6 1dc and 1ch sp and 5 rows to 4 in. (10 cm) over mesh patt using I/9 (5.50-mm) hook. Change hook size if necessary to obtain this gauge.

ABBREVIATIONS

ch = chain; **cont** = continue; **dc** = double crochet; **patt** = pattern; **sc** = single crochet; **sp(s)** = space(s); **ss** = slip stitch; **[ ]** = work instructions in brackets as directed.

NOTES

■ This stitch pattern is easy to do because, apart from the first row and the edge stitches, the hook is inserted into the spaces between the double crochet stitches.
■ There is no right or wrong side; the stitch pattern is reversible.

TIPS

■ It really is vital to make the starting chain very loose. Either pull each chain up until it is about ⅜ in. (1 cm) long, or if you find it difficult to keep the chain loops the same size, use a hook one, two, or even several sizes larger.

■ Although the number of rows to work is given, you don't need to count them; just work until you run out of yarn.

■ When making the wrap, you can join in a new ball of yarn anywhere in a row; simply knot the ends securely and continue working. Snipping off long ends level with the tags and tassels in the yarn is quicker than darning them in.

■ If you're not sure about working with such a heavily textured yarn, buy just one ball and make the scarf. Handle the yarn lightly, catching the core of the yarn and pulling through loosely as you make the stitches.

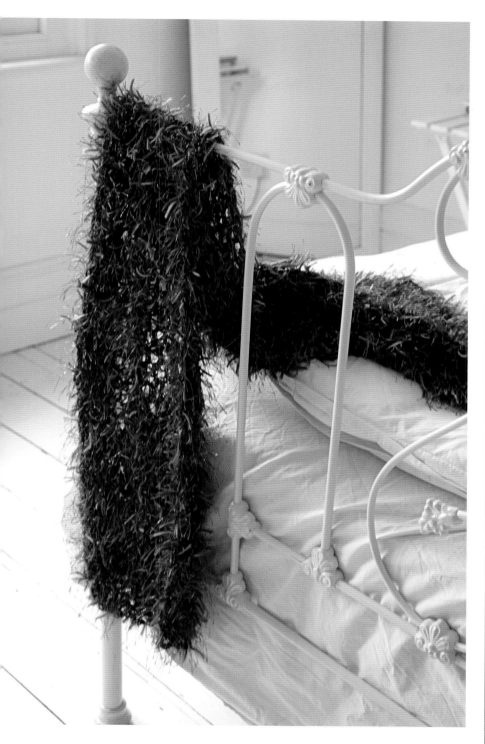

Throw on this skinny textured scarf to liven up a plain top, or wear it as an unusual belt to add some pizzazz to jeans.

SCARF AND WRAP

Make 10(54)ch.

Row 1 1dc in 6th ch from hook, [1ch, skip 1ch, 1dc in next ch] to end.

Row 2 1sc in first dc, 2ch, 1dc in first sp, [1ch, 1dc in next sp] to end, 1dc in 4th ch.

Row 3 1sc in first dc, 3ch, 1dc in first sp, [1ch, 1dc in next sp] to end, 1ch, 1dc in 2nd ch.

Row 4 1sc in first dc, 2ch, 1dc in first sp, [1ch, 1dc in next sp] to end, 1dc in 2nd ch. The 3rd and 4th rows form the mesh patt. Cont in patt for 64(67) more rows. Fasten off.

TO FINISH

Darn in ends.

Lacy Red Hat

All you have to do to make this lacy hat is crochet just five motifs, join them in a ring, fill in the top, add an edging, and it's ready to wear. Although the yarn is fine, this hat is quick to make because the motifs are very open—and it's so light, you can carry it along with you and crochet in the car or while waiting in line.

ESTIMATED TIME TO COMPLETE
Each motif takes 35 minutes; complete hat 4 hours.

ABOUT THIS YARN
Elle Crochet No. 5 is a smooth, lightweight, 100 percent acrylic yarn with approximately 273 yd. (250 m) to a 50-g ball.

SIZE
Fits average size head
Circumference 20½ in. (52 cm)

YOU WILL NEED
■ 1 x 50-g ball of Elle Crochet No. 5 in red, shade 09
■ B/1 (2.00-mm) crochet hook

GAUGE
Each motif measures 4 in. (10 cm) across using B/1 (2.00-mm) hook. Change hook size if necessary to obtain this size motif.

ABBREVIATIONS
ch = chain; **dc** = double; **3dctog** = leaving last loop of each st on hook, work 3dc, yo and pull through 4 loops on hook; **rep** = repeat; **RS** = right side; **sc** = single crochet; **sp(s)** = space(s); **ss** = slip stitch; **st(s)** = stitch(es); **tr** = triple; **2trtog** = leaving last loop of each st on hook, work 2tr, yo and pull through 3 loops on hook; **yo** = yarn over hook; [ ] = work instructions in brackets as directed.

TIPS
■ If you darn in the ends as you work, there will be no finishing to do!
■ To add sparkle to your lacy hat, investigate metallic filament at your local yarn shop. These fine strands will add shine and glitter, not weight, to your hat.

HAT MOTIF

Make 8ch, ss in first ch to form a ring.
Round 1 (RS) 4ch, 1tr in ring, 2ch, [2trtog in ring, 2ch] 11 times, ss in tr.
Round 2 Ss in first 2ch sp, 1ch, 1sc in same sp, 4ch, [1sc in next sp, 4ch] 11 times, ss in first sc.
Round 3 Ss in first 4ch sp, 1ch, 1sc in same sp, [* 12ch, 1sc in same 4ch sp, 5ch, 1sc in next 4ch sp *, 5ch, 1sc in foll 4ch sp] 5 times, rep from * to *, 2ch, 1dc in first sc.
Round 4 [6dc, 3ch, 6dc] in first 12ch sp, * 1sc in next 5ch sp, 5ch, 1sc in foll 5ch sp, [6dc, 3ch, 6dc] in next 12ch sp, rep from * 4 more times, 1sc in next 5ch sp, 2ch, 1dc in last dc of 3rd round.
Round 5 8ch, 1tr in same sp as join, [8ch, 1sc in next 3ch sp, 8ch, 1tr in next 5ch sp, 3ch, 1tr in same 5ch sp] 5 times, 8ch, 1sc in last 3ch sp, 8ch, ss in 5th ch.
Round 6 Ss in first 3ch sp, 1ch, [1sc, 5ch, 1sc] in same 3ch sp, * [1sc, 5ch, 1sc] 3 times in each of next two 8ch sps **, [1sc, 5ch, 1sc] in next 3ch sp, rep from * 4 times, then rep from * to **, ss in first sc. Fasten off.

BAND

Work 4 more motifs, joining 2nd, 3rd, and 4th motifs on the 6th round in an 8ch sp, 3ch sp and next 8ch sp along one straight edge by working [1sc in ch sp, 2ch, 1sc in first adjacent 5ch sp of previous motif, 2ch, 1sc in ch sp of motif] 7 times, then completing round. Leave two straight edges free at either side of joined edge. Join 5th motif to first and 4th motifs to form a ring.

TOP

With RS facing, join yarn in last free 5ch sp at right of a join between motifs.

Round 1 1ch, 1sc in same sp as join, [3ch, 1sc in next free sp] to end, 3ch, ss in first sc. 70 sps.

Round 2 Ss in first 3ch sp, 4ch, [1dc in next 3ch sp, 1ch] to end, ss in 3rd ch.

Round 3 2ch, 1dc in next 1ch sp, * [1ch, 1dc in next 1ch sp] 12 times **, 1ch, placing first part dc in next sp, 2nd part dc in next dc and 3rd part dc in foll 1ch sp, work 3dctog, rep from * 3 times, then rep from * to **, 1dc in next 1ch sp, ss in first dc. Working instructions in brackets one less time on each round and placing 2nd part of 3dctog in previous 3dctog, work in same way as 3rd round for 11 more rounds.

Round 15 2ch, 1dc in next 1ch sp, 1ch, [3dctog, 1ch] 4 times, 1dc in next 1ch sp, ss in first dc.

Round 16 1ch, 1sc in each 3dctog, ss in first sc. 5 sts. Fasten off.

Thread end of yarn through sts, draw up, and secure.

EDGING

With RS facing, join yarn in last free 5ch sp at right of a join between motifs.

Round 1 1ch, 1sc in same sp as join, [2sc in each 5ch sp] to end, 1sc in first 5ch sp, ss in first sc.

Round 2 1ch, 1sc in first sc, [1sc in each sc] to end, ss in first sc.

Round 3 1ch, 1sc in first sc, [5ch, skip 1sc, 1sc in next sc] to last sc, 5ch, skip last sc, ss in first sc. Fasten off. Darn in ends.

You'll need just one ball of yarn to make this pretty hat.

This simple hat can be
decorated with a crochet
flower in any color.

Cloche Hat with Flower

This pretty hat is just double crochet worked in rounds from the top down. There are five increase rounds; then you carry on straight. Darn in the ends, roll up the brim, and it's ready to wear. The yarn is chunky, so it works up quickly but is soft and supple with a pearly sheen that makes the stitches show up beautifully. The flower uses single, half-double, and double crochet and is so simple you'll want to make more than one!

ESTIMATED TIME TO COMPLETE
The hat took 1 hour and 20 minutes, plus 15 minutes for the flower. Total time taken, 1 hour 40 minutes.

ABOUT THIS YARN
Debbie Bliss Cashmerino Superchunky is a mix of 55 percent merino wool, 33 percent microfiber, and 12 percent cashmere. It has 82 yd. (75 m) to a 50-g ball.

SIZE
Circumference 22 in. (55.5 cm);
flower 4¼ in. (11 cm)

YOU WILL NEED
■ 2 x 100-g balls of Debbie Bliss Cashmerino Superchunky in cream, shade 01
■ K/10½ (7.00-mm) crochet hook

GAUGE
9 sts and 5 rows to 4 in. (10 cm) over double crochet using K/10½ (7.00-mm) hook. Change hook size if necessary to obtain this gauge.

ABBREVIATIONS
ch = chain stitch; **dc** = double crochet; **foll** = following; **hdc** = half-double crochet; **sc** = single crochet; **sp** = space; **ss** = slip stitch; **st(s)** = stitch(es); **[ ]** = work instructions in brackets as directed.

TIPS
■ When working double crochet in rounds, you will get a neater join if you work the first and second chains at the start of the round tightly and the third quite loosely. This will make it easier to slip the hook under both loops of the 3rd chain to work the step stitch at the end of the round.
■ Sew a pin on the back of the flower and use it as a corsage.

The 6th round forms double crochet. Cont in dc, work 10 more rounds.
Fasten off.
Darn in ends and roll up brim.

FLOWER

Wind yarn around finger to make a ring.
Round 1 1ch, 12sc in ring, pull end to close ring, ss in first sc. 12 sts.
Round 2 1sc in same place as ss, [3ch, skip 1sc, 1sc in next sc] 5 times, 3ch, skip 1sc, ss in first sc.
Round 3 [1sc, 1hdc, 1dc, 1hdc, 1sc] in each 3ch sp.
Round 4 Taking hook behind, ss around first sc of 2nd round, [5ch, ss around next sc of 2nd round] 5 times, 5ch, ss in first ss.
Round 5 [1sc, 1hdc, 3dc, 1hdc, 1sc] in each 5ch sp, ss in first dc.
Fasten off.
Darn in ends and sew on side of hat.

HAT

Wind yarn around finger to form a ring.
Round 1 3ch, 9dc in ring, pull end to close ring, ss in 3rd ch. 10 sts.
Round 2 3ch, 1dc in same place as ss, [2dc in each dc] to end, ss in 3rd ch. 20 sts.
Round 3 3ch, 1dc in same place as ss, [1dc in next dc, 2dc in foll dc] 9 times, 1dc in next dc, ss in 3rd ch. 30 sts.

Round 4 3ch, 1dc in same place as ss, [1dc in each of next 2dc, 2dc in foll dc] 9 times, 1dc in each of next 2dc, ss in 3rd ch. 40 sts.
Round 5 3ch, 1dc in same place as ss, [1dc in each of next 3dc, 2dc in foll dc] 9 times, 1dc in each of next 3dc, ss in 3rd ch. 50 sts.
Round 6 3ch, [1dc in each dc] to end, ss in 3rd ch.

Trapper Hat

Very thick yarn and a huge hook make fast work of this stylish hat. It is created entirely in single crochet, even the faux-fur trim. Start with a simple strip to go around the head, then join the ends and work the top of the hat in rounds. Add the earflaps and the contrast edging to finish.

ESTIMATED TIME TO COMPLETE
2 hours.

ABOUT THIS YARN
Rowan Big Wool is a soft merino wool yarn with 87 yd. (80 m) to a 100-g ball. Rowan Big Wool Tuft is 97 percent merino wool and 3 percent nylon, with approximately 27 yd. (25 m) to a 50-g ball. It has faux-fur tufts twisted into the yarn.

SIZE
Circumference 22 in. (56 cm)

YOU WILL NEED
- 2 x 100-g balls of Rowan Big Wool in Latte, shade 018 (A)
- 1 x 50-g ball of Rowan Big Wool Tuft in Frosty, shade 055 (B)
- M/13 (9.00-mm) crochet hook
- 2 buttons

GAUGE
7½ sts and 7 rows to 4 in. (10 cm) over single crochet using M/13 (9.00-mm) hook. Change hook size if necessary to obtain this gauge.

ABBREVIATIONS
ch = chain; **cont** = continue; **RS** = right side; **sc** = single crochet; **2sctog** = insert hook in first st and pull loop through, insert hook in second st and pull loop through, yo and pull through 3 loops on hook; **ss** = slip stitch; **st(s)** = stitch(es); **yo** = yarn over hook; **[ ]** = work instructions in brackets as directed.

BAND

Using A, make 11ch.
Row 1 1sc in 2nd ch from hook, [1sc in each ch] to end. 10 sts.
Row 2 1ch, [1sc in each sc] to end.
The 2nd row forms single crochet. Cont in sc, work 37 more rows. Join ends of band with sc by working each loop of starting ch with a sc of the last row. Do not fasten off.

CROWN

Round 1 (RS) Cont in A. 1ch, 1sc in each row-end, ss in first sc. 39 sts.
Round 2 1ch, 1sc in each sc to end, ss in first sc.
Round 3 1ch, 1sc in first sc, 2sctog, [1sc in next sc, 2sctog] to end, ss in first sc. 26 sts.
Round 4 1ch, 1sc in each sc to end, ss in first sc.

Round 5 1ch, 1sc in first sc, [2sctog] 12 times, 1sc in last sc, ss in first sc. 14 sts.
Round 6 1ch, 1sc in each sc to end, ss in first sc.
Round 7 1ch, [2sctog] 7 times.
Leaving a long end, fasten off. Thread end under the top loop of each st of last round, draw up to close top, and darn in end.

EARFLAPS

Left earflap Using A and with RS facing, join yarn in 13th row-end before center back join.
Row 1 1ch, 1sc in same row-end as joined yarn, 1sc in each of next 6 row-ends, turn. 7 sts. Work one row sc.
Row 3 1ch, 2sctog, 1sc in each of next 3sc, 2sctog. 5 sts. Work one row sc.
Row 5 1ch, 2sctog, 1sc in next sc, 2sctog. 3 sts. Work 1 row sc. Fasten off.
Right earflap Using A and with RS facing, join yarn in 7th row-end after center back join. Complete as given for left earflap.

TRIM

Using B, and with RS facing, join yarn at back seam between band and crown and work one round of surface sc around top of hat. Using B and with RS facing, join yarn at center back lower edge and work one round of sc in row ends all around band and earflap edges, omitting one row at each side of each earflap. Work 2nd round of sc. Fasten off.

TO FINISH

Darn in ends. Fold earflaps up and sew on the buttons to secure.

This simple hat is
incredibly easy to
make and wonderfully
warm to wear.

Beaded Beret

This beautiful beret is both effective and very simple to make. It's worked in rows using different height stitches to shape the segments. Adding the beads to outline the segments is easy; just thread them on and bring them up close between stitches on a single crochet row.

ESTIMATED TIME TO COMPLETE

3½ hours, including threading the beads

ABOUT THIS YARN

Debbie Bliss Cashmerino Chunky is a luxurious lightweight, super-smooth mix of 55 percent merino wool, 33 percent microfiber, and 12 percent cashmere. It has 71 yd. (65 m) to a 50-g ball.

SIZE

Fits average-size head
Circumference 19 in. (48 cm)

YOU WILL NEED

■ 3 x 50-g balls of Debbie Bliss Cashmerino Chunky in pale pink, shade 04
■ G/6 (4.50-mm) crochet hook
■ 492 medium-size glass beads

GAUGE

Each segment measures 2¼ in. (5.5 cm) at widest part, 1¼ in. (3 cm) at brim edge, 13 rows to 4 in. (10 cm) using a G/6 (4.50-mm) hook. Change hook size if necessary to obtain this gauge.

ABBREVIATIONS

ch = chain stitch; **dc** = double crochet; **hdc** = half-double crochet; **RS** = right side; **sc** = single crochet; **2sctog** = insert hook in first stitch and pull loop through, insert hook in 2nd stitch and pull loop through, yarn over hook and pull through 3 loops on hook; **ss** = slip stitch; **st(s)** = stitch(es); **[ ]** = work instructions in brackets as directed.

NOTES

■ Thread 203 beads on each of two balls of yarn and 58 beads on the third ball. Use beaded yarn for the segments and yarn without beads for top and brim edging.
■ The beads hang between stitches, so they are not included in stitch counts.

TIPS

■ To check your gauge, work the first segment. If it is the correct measurement, you can carry on. Try again with a smaller hook, if your segment was too large, or with a bigger hook, if your segment was too small.
■ If you want a beret without beads, simply omit them and work a plain sc row between segments.
■ Check that your beads have holes large enough to thread on to the yarn before buying them. If necessary, choose larger beads.
■ The exact number of beads is given, but if you are buying glass beads by weight, you'll probably find that 100 g will be enough. Plastic beads weigh less, so you may only need 50 g.
■ Try the beret on before working the brim edging. If you want a tighter fit, work fewer dc around the edge; if you want a looser fit, work more dc around edge.
■ The beret here uses pearly pink beads to match the yarn, but you could choose beads in a contrasting color or select colors to match a favorite outfit.

BERET

First segment Make 30ch.

Row 1 (RS) Bring a bead up close to the hook, 1sc in 2nd ch from hook, [bring a bead up close to hook, 1sc in next ch] to end. 29 sts.

Row 2 1ch, 1sc in each of first 5sc, 1hdc in each of next 3sc, 1dc in each of next 9sc, 1hdc in each of next 6sc, 1sc in each of next 3sc, ss in next sc, turn and leave 2sc.

Row 3 Ss in ss, 1sc in each of next 3sc, 1hdc in each of next 6hdc, 1dc in each of next 9dc, 1hdc in each of next 3hdc, 1sc in each of next 5sc.

Row 4 1ch, 1sc in each of next 5sc, 1hdc in each of next 3hc, 1dc in each of next 9dc, 1hdc in each of next 6hdc, 1sc in each of next 6 sts.

Row 5 1ch, [bring bead up close to hook, 1sc in next st] to end.

Rows 2 to 5 form the pattern.

2nd to 15th segments Patt 56 rows.

16th segment Work 2nd, 3rd and 4th row. Fasten off.

Close top Join back seam. With RS facing, join yarn at seam.

Round 1 Work 1sc in each segment, ss in first sc. 16 sts.

Round 2 1ch, [2sctog] 8 times, ss in first st. 8 sts.

Round 3 1ch, [2sctog] 4 times, ss in first st. 4 sts.

Fasten off.

Brim edging With RS facing, join yarn at the seam.

Round 1 Work 4sc in row-ends of each segment, ss in first sc, turn. 64 sts.

Round 2 Work 1sc in each sc to end, ss in first sc. Fasten off.

TO FINISH

At the top of the beret, sew 16 beads on the first round, 8 beads on the 2nd round and four beads on the 3rd round. Darn in ends.

Add a touch of luxury to any outfit with this pearly pastel beret.

Granny Square Gloves

Make gloves or fingerless mitts to match the Granny Square Hat on page 33. Use natural or blending shades, or have fun mixing and matching to use up even tiny scraps in a riot of color. Each glove is just two traditional granny squares joined together, then finished with a shell trim around the wrist and a choice of finger openings or single crochet fingers.

ESTIMATED TIME TO COMPLETE

Each granny square took about 20 minutes; the fingerless gloves took 4 hours; the gloves with fingers took 7 hours.

ABOUT THIS YARN

Use the same kind of pure wool and wool-mix DK/sport-weight yarn as for the Granny-Squares Hat on page 33.

SIZE

Fits average size hands

Around palm 8 in. (20 cm)

YOU WILL NEED

For the fingerless gloves

■ approximately 60 g of pure wool or wool-mix DK/sport-weight yarn in any colors

For the gloves with fingers

■ approximately 90 g of pure wool or wool-mix DK/sport-weight yarn in any colors you prefer

For both

■ E/4 (3.50-mm.) crochet hook

GAUGE

Granny square measures 3¼ x 3¼ in. (8 x 8 cm) using an E/4 (3.50-mm) hook. Change hook size if necessary to obtain this size square.

ABBREVIATIONS

beg = beginning; **ch** = chain; **cont** = continue; **dc** = double crochet; **dec** = decrease; **RS** = right side; **sc** = single crochet; **sp** = space; **ss** = slip stitch; **st(s)** = stitch(es); **WS** = wrong side; **[ ]** = work instructions in brackets as directed.

NOTES

■ The instructions do not give color changes, so change color whenever you wish.

■ To change colors when working the square, simply fasten off and join the new color in the corner space instead of working a slip stitch.

■ For fingerless mitts, fasten off after working the 2nd round of each finger and after working the 2nd round after the decrease round on each thumb.

TIPS

■ When working the single crochet rounds, remember to work the last loop of the last st of the round in the new color to make a neater join.

■ It's easier to work a slip stitch under both loops of the chain if the 3rd of the 3ch at the start of a double crochet round is worked loosely.

■ Try on the gloves after working the thumb-hole joins, just to make sure that you have a pair!

■ Have fun playing with the colors; for instance, you could work each finger in a different color.

■ Darn in ends as you work and when you finish the last round, you'll have just one end to darn in before you can wear your gloves.

■ It's quicker to use one color to work the granny square for the palm because there are no ends to deal with. Making the gloves in one color would be faster, but not as pretty.

■ If you have enough yarn, you could make the gloves longer in the wrist; just work more rounds of sc before finishing off with the shell edging.

■ For even faster fingerless gloves, fasten off at the top edge after the last round of sc, then try on the gloves and mark between your fingers. Take off the gloves and sew together at each mark to make finger holes.

■ If you want to change the length of the fingers, work more or fewer rounds, checking the fit as you go.

Turn simple granny squares into stylish gloves.

GRANNY SQUARE

Wind yarn around finger to form a ring.

Round 1 (RS) 5ch, [3dc in ring, 2ch] 3 times, 2dc in ring, pull end to close ring, ss in 3rd ch.

Round 2 Ss in first sp, 5ch, 3dc in first sp, 1ch, [3dc, 2ch, 3dc, 1ch] in each corner 2ch sp, 2dc in first sp, ss in 3rd ch.

Round 3 Ss in first sp, 5ch, 3dc in first sp, 1ch, [3dc in next 1ch sp, 1ch, 3dc, 2ch, 3dc in corner 2ch sp, 1ch] 3 times, 3dc in last 1ch sp, 1ch, 2dc in first sp, ss in 3rd ch.

Round 4 Ss in first sp, 5ch, 3dc in first sp, 1ch, [3dc in next 1ch sp, 1ch, 3dc in foll 1ch sp, 1ch, 3dc, 2ch, 3dc in corner 2ch sp, 1ch] 3 times, 3dc in next 1ch sp, 1ch, 3dc in last 1ch sp, 1ch, 2dc in first sp, ss in 3rd ch. Fasten off.

LEFT GLOVE

Make two granny squares, one for the back and one for the palm.

Back of hand Join yarn in one corner 2ch sp of first square. Work 3ch, then 1dc in each dc and each ch along one edge, ending with 1dc in corner sp. 17 sts. Fasten off.

Work a row of dc along opposite edge in the same way.

First joining row With WS together and back of glove facing you, join yarn to 3rd ch at beg of last row, 1sc in same place as join, 1ch, 1sc in corner sp of palm, [1ch, skip 1dc, 1sc in next dc of back, 1ch, skip one st, 1sc in next st of palm] 8 times, ending with a sc in corner sp of palm. Fasten off.

Thumb hole. 2nd joining row With back of glove facing, join yarn in corner sp opposite first side. With WS together, work as first side until 4th join in palm has been

completed. Fasten off. Skip next 7dc of back edge, join yarn in next dc, and work first join in center dc of last dc group of palm edge, 1ch, 1sc in last dc of back edge, 1ch, 1sc in corner sp of palm. Fasten off.

Top edge With palm facing, join yarn in first sp of square.

Round 1 (RS) 3ch, 1dc in each dc along top edge of palm square, 1dc in corner sp of palm square, 1dc in join, 2dc in row-end dc, 1dc in corner sp of back square, 1dc in each dc along top edge of back square, 1dc in corner sp of back square, 2dc in row-end dc, 1dc in join, ss in 3rd ch. 34 sts.

Round 2 1ch, 1sc in same place as ss, 1sc in each dc to end, ss in first sc.
Work 3 more rounds sc.

FINGERS

Little finger. Round 1 1ch, 1sc in same sc as ss, 1sc in each of next 2sc, 2ch, skip next 25sc, 1sc in each of next 6sc, ss in first sc.

Round 2 1ch, 1sc in each of first 3sc, 1sc in each ch, 1sc in each of next 6sc, ss in first sc. 11 sts. Cont in sc, work 8 more rounds.

Dec round 1ch, 1sc in first sc, [skip 1sc, 1sc in next sc] to end, ss in first sc. 6 sts. Fasten off.

Ring finger Join yarn in next sc of palm edge.

Round 1 1ch, 1sc in same sc as joined yarn, 1sc in each of next 2sc, 2ch, skip next 19sc, 1sc in each of next 3sc, 4sc in edge of little finger, ss in first sc.

Round 2 1ch, 1sc in each sc to ch, 1sc in each ch, 1sc in each sc to end, ss in first sc. 12 sts. Cont in sc, work 10 more rounds.

Dec round 1ch, 1sc in first sc, [skip 1sc, 1sc in next sc] to last sc, skip last sc, ss in first sc. 6 sts. Dec in same way on next round. 3 sts. Fasten off.

Middle finger Join yarn in next sc of palm edge.

Round 1 1ch, 1sc in same sc as joined yarn, 1sc in each of next 3sc, 2ch, skip next 11sc, 1sc in each of next 4sc, 4sc in edge of ring finger, ss in first sc.

Round 2 1ch, 1sc in each sc to ch, 1sc in

each ch, 1sc in each sc to end, ss in first sc. 14 sts. Cont in sc, work 11 more rounds. Dec in same way as ring finger on next round. 7 sts. Dec in same way as little finger on next round. 4 sts. Fasten off.

First finger Join yarn in next sc of palm edge.

Round 1 1ch, 1sc in same sc as joined yarn, 1sc in each of next 10sc, 4sc in edge of middle finger, ss in first sc. 15 sts.

Round 2 1ch, skip first sc, 1sc in each sc to end, ss in first sc. 14 sts.
Cont in sc, work 9 more rounds. Dec in same way as middle finger on next 2 rounds. 4 sts. Fasten off.

Thumb Join yarn at palm side lower edge of opening, Work 22sc around opening, ss in first sc. Work one more round sc.

Dec round 1ch, 1sc in first sc, [skip 1sc, 1sc in next sc] twice, 1sc in each of next 10sc, [skip 1sc, 1sc in next sc] 3 times, skip last sc, ss in first sc. 16 sts. Cont in sc, work 9 more rounds. Dec in same way as ring finger on next 2 rounds. 4 sts. Fasten off.

Wrist Work around lower edge in same way as given for top edge until 5 rounds of sc have been completed.

Next round 1ch, 1sc in first sc, skip 1sc, 1sc in each sc to last sc, skip 1sc, ss in first sc. 32 sts.

Shell edging [Skip 1sc, 5dc in next sc, skip 1sc, ss in next sc] 8 times. Fasten off.

RIGHT GLOVE

Work as given for left glove until first joining row of back and palm has been completed. For the thumb hole, work the short join, then leaving 7dc of edge, work the longer join.

Work the top edge as given for left glove but fasten off after completing the rounds of sc.

Fingers Count from end of round and join yarn in 12th sc.

Little finger 1ch, 1sc in same sc as join, 1sc in each of next 8sc, 2ch, ss in first sc.
Complete little finger as left glove, then work remaining fingers to match.

Granny Square Hat

Whip up six granny squares and join them together to make this fun hat. If you have lots of yarn to choose from, you can work out a planned color scheme; or with leftover scrap yarns enjoy combining the colors freestyle.

ESTIMATED TIME TO COMPLETE
5 hours

ABOUT THIS YARN
Use pure-wool or wool-rich-mix DK/sport-weight yarns in any colors you like. Just make sure that the yarns can all be washed the same way.

SIZE
Circumference 22 in. (56 cm)

YOU WILL NEED
- Approximately 70 g of pure-wool or wool-mix DK/sport-weight yarn in black (A)
- 70 g of pure-wool or wool mix DK/sport-weight yarn in colors of your choice (B)
- E/4 (3.50-mm) crochet hook

GAUGE
Each granny square measures 3¼ x 3¼ in. (8 x 8 cm) using an E/4 (3.50-mm) hook. Change hook size if necessary to obtain this size square.

ABBREVIATIONS
ch = chain; **cont** = continue; **dc** = double crochet; **3dctog** = leaving last loop of each st on hook, work 3dc, yarn over hook and pull through 4 loops on hook; **RS** = right side; **sc** = single crochet; **sp** = space; **ss** = slip stitch; **st(s)** = stitch(es); [ ] = work instructions in brackets as directed.

NOTE
See notes and tips for Granny Square Gloves on page 30.

TIPS
- Although just three colors are used for the hat in the picture, you could choose one main color, then use as many bright colors as you like for the contrast.
- If you're not sure about a color scheme, put your scrap yarns out and sort through them to find colors that go together. Natural and brown gives a classic effect with cream as a main color, or you could work the hat in different tones of one color.
- For a smaller hat, use a smaller size hook to reduce the size of the granny squares. If you make the squares 2¾ x 2¾ in. (7 x 7 cm), your hat will measure approximately 20 in. (50 cm) around the band.

BAND
Mixing colors as desired and working last round in B, make six granny squares as given for gloves on page 32. Lay squares in a row with RS facing up.
Joining row (RS) Join A in corner sp of first square, 1sc in corner sp of first square, 1ch, 1sc in corresponding corner sp of 2nd square, [1ch, skip one st, 1sc in next st of first square, 1ch, 1sc in corresponding st of 2nd square, 1ch, skip one st, 1sc in next sp of first square, 1ch, 1sc in corresponding sp of 2nd square] four times. Fasten off.
Join 3rd, 4th, 5th, and 6th squares in this way, then join 6th square to first square.

CROWN
Join A to center sp of first motif.

Round 1 (RS) 1ch, 1sc in same sp, 1sc in each of next 8 sts or sps, [17 sc across next square] 5 times, 1sc in each of next 8 sps or sts, ss in first sc. 102 sc.
Change the colors as desired to work the sc rounds.
Round 2 1ch, 1sc in each sc to end, ss in first sc.
Round 2 forms sc. Cont in sc, work 2 more rounds. Cont in A.
Round 5 3ch, 1dc in each of next 6sc, 3dctog, [1dc in each of next 14sc, 3dctog] 5 times, 1dc in each of last 7sc, ss in 3rd ch. 90 sts.

Round 6 3ch, 1dc in each of next 5dc, 3dctog, [1dc in each of next 12dc, 3dctog] 5 times, 1dc in each of last 6dc, ss in 3rd ch. 78 sts.

Round 7 3ch, 1dc in each of next 4dc, 3dctog, [1dc in each of next 10dc, 3dctog] 5 times, 1dc in each of last 5dc, ss in 3rd ch. 66 sts.

Changing colors as desired, work 3 rounds sc, then cont in A.

Round 11 3ch, 1dc in each of next 3sc, 3dctog, [1dc in each of next 8sc, 3dctog] 5 times, 1dc in each of last 4sc, ss in 3rd ch. 54 sts.

Round 12 3ch, [1dc in each dc] to end, ss in 3rd ch.

Round 13 3ch, 1dc in each of next 2dc,

3dctog, [1dc in each of next 6dc, 3dctog] 5 times, 1dc in each of last 3dc, ss in 3rd ch. 42 sts.

Changing colors as desired, work 3 rounds sc, then cont in A.

Round 17 3ch, 1dc in next sc, 3dctog, [1dc in each of next 4sc, 3dctog] 5 times, 1dc in each of last 2sc, ss in 3rd ch. 30 sts.

Round 18 As 12th round.

Round 19 3ch, 3dctog, [1dc in each of next 2dc, 3dctog] 5 times, 1dc in last dc, ss in 3rd ch. 18 sts.

Rounds 20 and 21 As Round 12.

Leaving a long end, fasten off. Thread end through tops of stitches, draw up, and secure.

TO FINISH

Complete lower edge of band by working first round as given for crown. Then, changing colors as desired, and decreasing two stitches on first round, work five more rounds sc and one round of shell edging as given at end of left glove on page 32. Make two 6-in. (15-cm)-long fat tassels; sew on top of hat.

Raid your yarn supply for this fun hat. Instructions for the gloves are on pages 30–32.

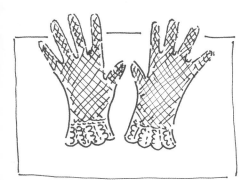

Black Lace Gloves

These gloves are just like the ones Grandma might have worn—but although they look authentic, the stitches are really simple. The two-row edging pattern has two crochet fans at the cuff edge, with double crochet and chain mesh at the wrist edge. The main part of the glove is worked in the round with the right side facing you all the time. The double crochet and chain mesh pattern is easy to work and easy to shape. You can take the time to make the gloves or make stylish fingerless mittens by working the edging and hand, then fastening off and stitching between the fingers.

ESTIMATED TIME TO COMPLETE

7 hours

ABOUT THIS YARN

Sirdar Town and Country 4ply is a smooth hard-wearing yarn originally made for knitting socks. It's a mix of 75 percent wool and 25 percent nylon with approximately 224 yd. (205 m) to a 50-g ball.

SIZE

Around palm 7½ in. (19 cm); **length** (excluding cuff) 8½ in. (21.5 cm)

YOU WILL NEED

- 1 x 50-g ball of Sirdar Town and Country 4ply in black, shade 151
- B/1 (2.00-mm) crochet hook

GAUGE

12 rows in edging patt measure 3½ in. (9 cm) at wrist edge and 4 in. (10 cm) at cuff edge, 13 1dc and 1ch sps and 15 rows to 4 in. (10 cm) over lace mesh patt when slightly stretched, using B/1 (2.00-mm) hook. Change hook size if necessary to obtain this gauge.

ABBREVIATIONS

ch = chain; **cont** = continue; **dc** = double crochet; **2dctog** = leaving last loop of each st on hook, work 2dc, yo and pull through 3 loops on hook; **3dctog** = leaving last loop of each st on hook, work 3dc, yo and pull through 4 loops on hook; **foll** = following; **patt** = pattern; **rep** = repeat; **RS** = right side; **sp(s)** = space(s); **ss** = slip stitch; **st(s)** = stitch(es); **yo** = yarn over hook; **[ ]** = work instructions in brackets as directed.

NOTE

The length of the hand and the fingers can be adjusted by trying the glove on and working more or fewer rounds before or between the shaping rounds.

TIPS

- The edging pattern for the right glove is reversed, so the right side of the pattern is mirror image when the gloves are worn. If you prefer, you could work the right glove edging in the same way as the left glove edging and turn it inside out.
- When making 4ch at the beginning of a mesh pattern round, work the 3rd chain slightly loosely; this will make it easier to insert the hook when joining at the end of the round.
- Keep the chain stitches between the doubles fairly loose so the mesh pattern is square. If your chain stitches are very tight, the mesh will be less flexible; if you really can't keep the mesh square with just one chain, it might be better to work 2 chains tightly instead.

LEFT GLOVE

Cuff edging Make 17ch.

Row 1 1dc in 7th ch from hook, 1ch, skip 1ch, 1dc in next ch, 2ch, skip 3ch, * 1dc in next ch, 3ch, 1dc in same ch as last dc *, 2ch, skip 3ch, rep from * to * in last ch.

Row 2 (RS) 3ch, 9dc in first 3ch sp, 7dc in next 3ch sp, [1dc in next dc, 1ch] twice, 1dc in 3rd ch.

Row 3 4ch, 1dc in next dc, 1ch, 1dc in foll dc, 2ch, skip first 3dc of 7dc group, * [1dc, 3ch, 1dc] in next dc *, 2ch, skip first 3dc of

9dc group, rep from * to *.

Rows 2 and 3 form the edging patt for left glove. Work 20 more rows.

Join in a round. Next row 3ch, 5dc in first 3ch sp, * work next dc until there are 2 loops on hook, insert hook in corresponding sp of first row, yo and pull through all loops on hook *, 3dc in same 3ch sp, 3dc in next 3ch sp, rep from * to *, 3dc in same 3ch sp, [rep from * to * to join next dc to ch at base of corresponding dc of first row, ss in next ch] twice, rep from * to * to join 3rd ch of previous row to last ch of first row.

Hand. Round 1 (RS) 4ch, [1dc in next ch, 1ch, 1dc in next dc, 1ch] to end, ss in 3rd ch. 24 1dc and 1ch sps.

Round 2 4ch, [1dc in next dc, 1ch] to end, ss in 3rd ch.

Round 2 forms lacy mesh patt.

Patt 2 more rounds.

Thumb gusset. Round 1 4ch, [1dc in next dc, 1ch] 9 times, [1dc, 1ch] twice in next dc, [1dc in next dc, 1ch] 13 times, ss in 3rd ch.

Round 2 4ch, [1dc in next dc, 1ch] 9 times, [1dc, 1ch] twice in each of next 2dc, [1dc in next dc, 1ch] 13 times, ss in 3rd ch.

Round 3 4ch, [1dc in next dc, 1ch] 9 times, [1dc, 1ch] twice in next dc, [1dc in next dc, 1ch] twice, [1dc, 1ch] twice in foll dc, [1dc in next dc, 1ch] 13 times, ss in 3rd ch.

Round 4 4ch, [1dc in next dc, 1ch] 9 times,

[1dc, 1ch] twice in next dc, [1dc in next dc, 1ch] 4 times, [1dc, 1ch] twice in next dc, [1dc in next dc, 1ch] 13 times, ss in 3rd ch.

Round 5 4ch, [1dc in next dc, 1ch] 9 times, [1dc, 1ch] twice in next dc, [1dc in next dc, 1ch] 6 times, [1dc, 1ch] twice in next dc, [1dc in next dc, 1ch] 13 times, ss in 3rd ch. 33 1dc and 1ch sps.

Patt 4 rounds.

Shape thumb hole. Next round 4ch, [1dc in next dc, 1ch] 9 times, yo, insert hook in next dc and in foll 9th dc, yo and pull through [yo and pull through 2 loops] twice, 1ch, 1dc in same place as join, 1ch, [1dc in next dc, 1ch] 13 times, ss in 3rd ch. 25 1dc and 1ch sps.

Patt 3 rounds.

Little finger. Round 1 4ch, [1dc, 1ch] in each of first 3dc, skip 18dc, [1dc, 1ch] in each of last 3dc, ss in 3rd ch. 7 1dc and 1ch sps.

Patt 5 rounds.

Close top. 2ch, [2dctog] 3 times. Fasten off.

Ring finger. Round 1 With palm facing, join yarn in same dc as 3rd dc of first round of little finger, 4ch, [1dc, 1ch] in each of next 3dc, skip 12dc, [1dc 1ch] in each of last 3 free dc, [1dc 1ch] in same dc as 4th dc of Round 1 of little finger, ss in 3rd ch. 8 1dc and 1ch sps.

Patt 7 rounds.

Close top. 2ch, [2dctog] twice, 3dctog. Fasten off.

Middle finger With palm facing, join yarn in same dc as 3rd dc of Round 1 of ring finger, skipping 6dc, work Round 1 as given for ring finger. Patt 8 rounds.

Close top As ring finger.

Forefinger With palm facing, join yarn in same dc as 3rd dc of Round 1 of middle finger, 4ch, [1dc, 1ch] in each of next 6dc, 1dc in same dc as 4th dc of Round 1 of middle finger, ss in 3rd ch. 8 1dc and 1ch sps. Complete as given for ring finger.

Thumb. Round 1 With palm facing, join yarn in same dc as joined dc at inner edge of thumb, 4ch, [1dc, 1ch] in each of next 8dc, ss in 3rd ch. 9 1dc and 1ch sps. Patt 5 rounds.

Close top 2ch, 2dctog, [3dctog] twice. Fasten off.

RIGHT GLOVE

Cuff edging. Make 20ch.

Row 1 1dc in 8th ch from hook, 2ch, skip 3ch, [1dc, 3ch, 1dc] in next ch, 2ch, skip 3ch, [1dc in next ch, 1ch] twice, 1dc in last ch.

Row 2 4ch, 1dc in next dc, 1ch, 1dc in foll dc, 7dc in 3ch sp, 10dc in last sp.

Row 3 Ss in each of first 7dc, 6ch, 1dc in same place as last ss, 2ch, skip first 3dc of 7dc group, [1dc, 3ch, 1dc] in next dc, 2ch, skip 3dc, [1dc, 1ch] in each of next 2dc, 1dc in 3rd ch.

Rows 2 and 3 form edging patt for right glove. Complete edging as given for left glove, reversing joining row. Fasten off.

Hand. Join yarn in first ch at cuff edge. Complete to match left glove, reversing the placing of the thumb gusset by working 13dc and 1ch sps before increasing and starting rounds for fingers with the back of the hand facing you.

TO FINISH

Thread ends at top of fingers and thumbs through sts, draw up, and secure. Stitch between base of fingers to close gaps. Darn in ends.

Add a little drama
to any outfit with
these vintage-style
lacy gloves.

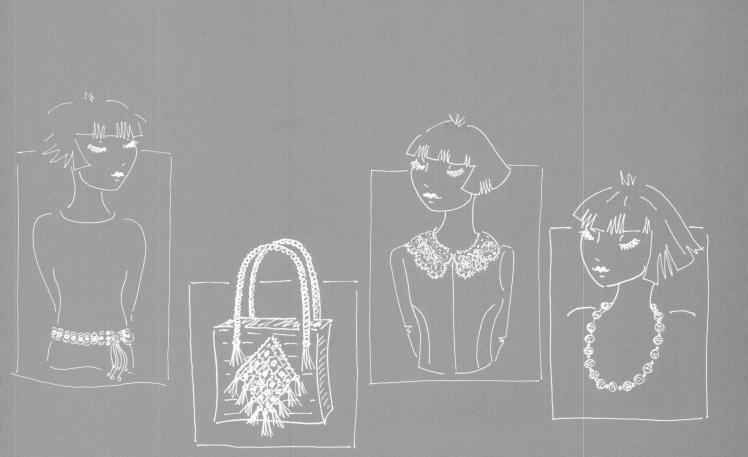

Accessories

String Bag

Made entirely from ordinary string, this boxy little tote is created with just four flat pieces of single crochet. The knotted decoration and handles are easy to do; they're worked using flat knots, which are simply square knots tied around a core.

ESTIMATED TIME TO COMPLETE
5 hours to crochet the bags, plus 2 hours to make up and add decoration.

ABOUT THIS YARN
The natural cream-colored string used for the bag is 100 percent cotton with a glazed finish and is slightly thicker than a sport-weight yarn, with approximately 109 yd. (100 m) to 3 oz. (84 g). The knotted decoration uses a heavier weight string, similar to Aran yarn, though denser, with approximately 66 yd. (60 m) to 3 oz. (84 g).

SIZE
Width 10 in. (25.5 cm); **length** 9½ in. (24 cm)

YOU WILL NEED
- 408 yd. (375 m) of thin cotton parcel string in cream
- 66 yd. (60 m) of thicker cotton parcel string in natural
- E/4 (3.50-mm) crochet hook
- blunt-pointed needle

GAUGE
15 sts and 18 rows to 4 in. (10 cm) over single crochet using E/4 (3.50-mm) hook. Change hook size if necessary to obtain this gauge.

ABBREVIATIONS
ch = chain; **sc** = single crochet; **[ ]** = work instructions in brackets as directed.

NOTES
- Buy a large spool of thin string, even if it is more than you need, so you'll have fewer ends to darn in. If you use small balls of string, join in at the start of a row so the ends can be hidden in the edging.
- Amounts given are approximate because string can vary.
- If you want a plain bag, you won't need the contrast string. Omit the knotted decoration and add braided or crochet handles.

TIP
To decorate your bag with flowers instead of knots, crochet motifs from the Irish Lace Pillow on page 138, or from the Rosebud Hairband on page 84 and sew them on.

BACK AND FRONT
Using the thinner string, make 41ch.
Row 1 1sc in 2nd ch from hook, [1sc in each ch] to end. 40 sc.
Row 2 1ch, [1sc in each sc] to end.
Row 2 forms single crochet. Work 42 more rows sc. Fasten off.
Work 2nd piece in the same way.

SIDE PANELS
Panel 1 Make 7ch.
Work Row 1 as given for back and front. 6sc.
Work 63 rows sc. Fasten off.
Panel 2 Work as Panel 1 but do not fasten off. Join last row of Panel 1 to last row of Panel 2 with sc. Fasten off.

EDGING
Placing chain edge of back and front at top, matching rows at sides and rows to stitches along lower edge, insert hook one stitch in from edge each time to join back and front to side panels with a row of sc. Fasten off and darn in ends.

KNOTTED DECORATION
Using the thicker string, cut 4 lengths, each 2¾ yd. (2.5 m) long. Fold 2 lengths in half and loop through on Row 11 down from top

This handy bag is just right for carrying your current crochet project.

between 17th and 18th stitches, and 2 between 23rd and 24th stitches, 14 rows down from top edge. Use 4 strands from center and 4 new strands to work 2 flat knots at each side.

3rd, 4th, and 5th lines of knots Using slightly shorter lengths of string for each group of 4 strands and spacing the new strands 3 rows down and 2 stitches out each time, join in and work 2 flat knots 3 times on 3rd line, 4 times on 4th line, and 5 times on 5th line.

6th, 7th, 8th, 9th lines of knots Leaving 4 strands at each side each time, work 2 flat knots 4 times on 6th line, 3 times on 7th line, twice on 8th line, and once on 9th line. Thread each group of 4 strands through between adjacent stitches to hold the last 4 lines of knots flat on the front of the bag. To finish each group of ends in a tassel, fold two of the ends and loop them through again to make 6 shorter lengths. Wrap the two longer ends around close to the bag, knot to secure, then thread a blunt-pointed needle with the ends to take them back through the bag, out again, and down through the wrapping. When all tassels have been made, trim ends.

HANDLES

For each handle Cut 6 lengths of thicker string for the core, each 39 1/2 in. (100 cm) long. Cut 4 lengths of thin string, each 2 3/4 yd. (2.5 m) long. Line up ends of both strings and tie in a firm overhand knot about 3 1/4 in. (8 cm) from the end. Use the thinner string to cover the core with flat knots, ending with an overhand knot 3 1/4 in. (8 cm) from end. Sew handles on each side of bag. Trim ends.

edge of front between 19th and 20th stitches, fold and loop through remaining 2 lengths between 21st and 22nd stitches, making 2 groups of 4 strands.

First flat knot Leaving a loop at top right, take the first 2 strands on the right over in front of the center 4 strands and under the last 2 strands on the left, then take these last 2 strands on the left behind the center 4 strands and out through the loop of 2 strands on the right. Pull ends gently to tighten first

half of knot. The outer strands have changed places. Leaving a loop out to the left, take the last 2 strands on the left over in front of the center 4 strands and under the last 2 strands on the right, then take these last 2 strands on the right behind the center 4 strands and out through the loop of 2 strands on the left. Pull ends to tighten completed knot. Work another flat knot using the same strands.

2nd line of knots Cut 4 more slightly shorter lengths of string and loop 2 through

Black Lace Bag

The bold, lacy pattern for the side panels is worked in rows using just chain, double, and triple crochet, with the occasional longer stitch. The pattern is arranged on the half drop, so you quickly get accustomed to the repeat. The silk lining panels are stiffened with fusible webbing, then the lacy side panels are stretched over them, giving the bag a boxy shape.

ESTIMATED TIME TO COMPLETE

6 hours

ABOUT THIS YARN

Sirdar Pure Cotton 4ply is a firm, smooth 100 percent cotton yarn with 370 yd. (338 m) to a 100-g ball.

SIZE

Width (at top edge) 9½ in. (24 cm); **height** 8¼ in. (21 cm)

YOU WILL NEED

- 1 x 100-g ball of Sirdar Pure Cotton 4ply in black, shade 041
- C/2 (2.50-mm) crochet hook
- 20 x 22-in. (50 x 56-cm) piece of red silk dupioni
- 22 x 10-in. (56 x 25-cm) piece of ultrahold fusible webbing
- magnetic bag catch
- black and red sewing thread and sharp sewing needle
- 33½-in. (84-cm) length of plastic-coated wire

GAUGE

One repeat measures 2½ in. (6 cm) across, 8 rows to 2¾ in. (7 cm), when pressed using a C/2 (2.50-mm) hook. Change hook size if necessary to obtain this gauge.

ABBREVIATIONS

ch = chain; **cont** = continue; **dc** = double crochet; **foll** = following; **rep** = repeat; **RS** = right side; **sc** = single crochet; **ss** = slip stitch; **st(s)** = stitch(es); **tr** = triple; **[ ]** = work instructions in brackets as directed.

SIDE PANELS

(Make 2) Make 50ch.

Row 1 (RS) 1sc in 2nd ch from hook, [1sc in each ch] to end. 49 sts.

Row 2 1ch, 1sc in first sc, 1sc in each of next 2sc, [* 4ch, skip 3sc, 1dc in next sc, 4ch, skip 3sc *, 1sc in each of next 5sc] 3 times, rep from * to *, 1sc in each of last 3sc.

Row 3 1ch, 1sc in first sc, 1sc in next sc, [* 3ch, 4dc in next 4ch sp, 1ch, 4dc in foll 4ch sp, 3ch *, skip 1sc, 1sc in each of next 3sc] 3 times, rep from * to *, skip 1sc, 1sc in each of last 2sc.

Row 4 1sc in first sc, 5ch, [4dc in next 3ch sp, 3ch, 1tr in 1ch sp, 3ch, 4dc in foll 3ch sp, 3ch, skip 1sc, 1dc in next sc, 3ch] 4 times, omitting last 3ch.

Row 5 1sc in first dc, 2ch, [4dc in next 3ch sp, 3ch, 1sc in foll 3ch sp, 1sc in tr, 1sc in next 3ch sp, 3ch, 4dc in foll 3ch sp, 1ch] 4 times, omitting last ch, 1dc in 2nd ch.

Row 6 1sc in first dc, 2ch, 1dc in same dc as sc, [* 4ch, 1sc in next 3ch sp, 1sc in each of next 3sc, 1sc in foll 3ch sp, 4ch *, 4dc in 1ch sp] 3 times, rep from * to *, 2dc in 2nd ch.

Row 7 1sc in first dc, 2ch, [4dc in next 4ch sp, 3ch, skip 1sc, 1sc in each of next 3sc, 3ch, 4dc in next 4ch sp, 1ch] 4 times, omitting last ch, 1dc in 2nd ch.

Row 8 1sc in first dc, 6ch, [* 4dc in next 3ch sp, 3ch, 1dc in center sc, 3ch, 4dc in foll 3ch sp, 3ch *, 1tr in 1ch sp, 3ch] 3 times, rep from * to *, 1tr in 2nd ch.

Row 9 1ch, 1sc in tr, 1sc in first 3ch sp, [* 3ch, 4dc in next 3ch sp, 1ch, 4dc in foll 3ch sp, 3ch, 1sc in next 3ch sp *, 1sc in tr, 1sc in foll 3ch sp] 3 times, rep from * to *, 1sc in 3rd ch.

Row 10 1ch, 1sc in first sc, 1sc in next sc, 1sc in first 3ch sp, [* 4ch, 4dc in 1ch sp, 4ch, 1sc in next 3ch sp*, 1sc in each of next 3sc, 1sc in foll 3ch sp] 3 times, rep from * to *, 1sc in each of last 2sc.

Work Rows 3 to 10 again, then Rows 3 to 9.

Last row 1ch, 1sc in first sc, 1sc in next sc, [* 4sc in 3ch sp, 1sc in each of next 4dc, 1sc in 1ch sp, 1sc in each of foll 4dc, 4sc in 3ch sp *, 1sc in each of next 3sc] 3 times, rep from * to *, 1sc in each of last 2sc. Fasten off.

HANDLES

(Make 2) Make 5ch, ss in first ch to form a ring. Work 7sc in ring. Cont in sc working in a spiral until handle measures 16 in. (40 cm). Fasten off.

LINING

Press side panels. Fold silk in half, place starting chain edge (top) of one side panel on fold and use as a template to cut 2 double pieces of silk lining with a ½-in. (1-cm) seam allowance at sides and lower edge. Cut fusible webbing to exact size of side panels. Open out folded lining and fuse webbing to WS of each piece, from fold line to lower edge. Remove backing paper from webbing. Put one half of the bag catch onto the webbing, just below the fold line on each side and centered. Fold the other half of the lining over the catch and fuse in place over the entire area, working carefully around the catch. Make a tiny rolled hem along the raw edges. Repeat for the other lining panel.

GUSSET

With RS of one side panel facing, join yarn to top left starting ch.

Row 1 Work 44sc down left side edge, 1sc in each of 81sc along lower edge and 44sc up right side edge. 169 sts.

Row 2 1ch, [1sc around stem of each sc] to end.

Row 3 1ch, [1sc in each sc] to end.

Cont in sc, work 2 more rows. Fasten off. Work 2nd side to match; do not fasten off.

TO FINISH

Sew edges of linings to side panels. Return to 2nd side of gusset, with RS facing and working through one stitch from each side each time, join last row of each side of gusset with sc. Fasten off and darn in ends. Cut plastic-coated wire in half, turn wire up at each end, and insert one piece in each handle. Sew handles on bag.

You can match the color of the bag's lining to your favorite dress or shoes.

Leather-and-Beads Belt

This attractive belt may look complex, but all you need to do is work a simple chain and two rows of single crochet, then add some ties and— voilà—you're finished.

ESTIMATED TIME TO COMPLETE
To crochet the belt takes 1 hour, plus 30 minutes to add the ties.

ABOUT THIS YARN
This kind of narrow round leather thong is available from jewelry suppliers. It is often sold in 1-yd. (1-m) lengths to hang pendants on, but you will need a continuous length because it would be messy and wasteful if you had to keep dealing with ends. The belt is in a natural tan color but thong is also available in brown and black.

SIZES
Width 1½ in. (3.5 cm); **length** (excluding ties) 33(**36¼**:38) in. [84(**92**:97) cm]
Figures in parentheses refer to larger sizes; one figure refers to all sizes.

YOU WILL NEED
■ 1 x 27-yd. (25-m) spool of ⅛ in. (2 mm) wide leather thong
■ 84(**89**:93) wooden beads
■ H/8 (5.00-mm) crochet hook

GAUGE
8 sts to 4 in. (10 cm) over beaded chain using H/8 (5.00-mm) hook. Change hook size if necessary to obtain this gauge.

ABBREVIATIONS
ch = chain; **sc** = single crochet; **WS** = wrong side

NOTES
■ Thread 65(**71**:75) beads onto the leather thong before starting to crochet.
■ The hook size given as a guide may seem quite small for the size of the stitches but the leather is so springy that the stitches open out and are very round. To measure your gauge, work several beaded chains then lay the chain flat, perhaps getting someone to hold down the other end because it will want to curl. If you don't get 8 beaded chains to 4 in. (10 cm), carefully undo the chain and try again, using a larger hook if your chain was less than 4 in. (10 cm) or a smaller hook if it was more.
■ Check for loose stitches as you work. There's no need to pull back, just ease any loose strands through with your fingers.

TIPS
■ You can take the curl out of the ties and flatten the belt by pressing gently with a steam iron.
■ If the beads are not waterproof, varnish them and leave to dry before making the belt.
■ Threading the beads isn't fiddly. The leather is stiff so you can just pick up a bead and slide it on.
■ Put the beads in a flat dish; it will be easier to pick them up, and you are less likely to spill them.
■ Instead of wooden beads, you could use glass or metal beads.

BELT
Center chain Put a slip knot on the hook and make 1ch, sliding a bead up close each time, make 65(**71**:75)ch, then make 1ch, turn.
Round 1 (WS) Working into top loop of each ch for first side and bottom loop for 2nd side, work 1sc in each ch to end.
To fasten off, leaving a 4-in. (10-cm) end, cut thong and pull end through last sc, then take end under top loops of first sc and back down through last sc before weaving it in firmly behind stitches.

TO FINISH
Weave starting end through stitches on WS. Cut six 29½-in. (75-cm) lengths of thong, fold in half, and loop three through the stitches at each narrow end of the belt. Thread both ends of each tie through a bead and push up close to end of belt to keep ties in place. Thread a bead on the end of each tie and knot to secure bead.

This striking belt is made using thin leather thong and wooden beads.

Victorian-Style Collar

This airy, authentic-looking lace collar is simple to make. It begins with a picot row because it's easier to work into and between picots than to count fine chains. The motifs and the edging pattern use the simplest stitches, and the pattern is organized to work into spaces not chain to make it easy on the eyes despite the fineness of the lace.

ESTIMATED TIME TO COMPLETE
Each motif takes 15 minutes, collar 7½ hours.

ABOUT THIS YARN
You can use any fine crochet cotton to make the collar—the original used approximately half of a 20-count (equivalent to 2ply), 100 percent cotton thread, with 436 yd. (400 m) to a 50-g ball.

SIZE
Neck edge circumference (adjustable) 21½ in. (55 cm)

YOU WILL NEED
- 1 x 25-g ball of 20-count crochet cotton in white
- No. 12 steel (0.75-mm) crochet hook
- spray starch or spray sizing

GAUGE
6 picots on first row, and 11 spaces on 2nd row measure 2 in. (5 cm) along shorter edge of neckband, and each motif measures 1¼ in. (4.5 cm) across, all when pressed, using No. 12 steel (0.75-mm) hook. Change hook size if necessary to obtain this size motif.

ABBREVIATIONS
ch = chain; **dc** = double crochet; **2dctog** = leaving last loop of each stitch on the hook, work two dc, yo and pull through 3 loops on hook; **3dctog** leaving last loop of each stitch on hook, work 3 dc, yo and pull through 4 loops on hook; **rep** = repeat; **RS** = right side; **sc** = single crochet; **sp(s)** = space(s); **ss** = slip stitch; **st(s)** = stitch(es); **yo** = yarn over hook; **[ ]** = work instructions in brackets as directed.

NOTES
- You can adjust the collar to fit around a smaller or larger neckline. Work more or fewer picot loops on the first row to of the neckband to fit around the neckline of your garment and adjust the 2nd row to a multiple of 11 spaces. Make one motif for each 11 spaces to join along the band on the first row of the edging.
- For a heavier weight cotton, adjust the hook size to obtain a fabric that feels right, then adjust the length of the neckband as described above.

NECKBAND
Row 1 5ch, 1dc in first ch, [6ch, 1dc in 5th ch from hook] 54 times. 55 picots.
Work along straight edge.
Row 2 (RS) 5ch, 1dc in first picot sp, [2ch, 1dc over ch between picots, 2ch 1dc in next picot sp] to last picot sp, 2ch, 1dc in first ch. 110 sps.
Row 3 1ch,1sc in first dc, [5ch, 1sc] in each sp to end, working last dc in 3rd ch. Fasten off.

MOTIF
Make 8ch, ss in first ch to form a ring.
Round 1 (RS) 1ch, [1sc in ring, 4ch] 7 times, 1sc in ring, 2ch, 1dc in first sc.
Round 2 3ch, 2dctog in dc sp, [4ch, 3dctog in next sp] 7 times, 2ch, 1dc in 2dctog.
Round 3 3ch, 2dctog in dc sp, [4ch, 3dctog] twice in each of next 7 sps, 4ch, 3dctog in first sp, 2ch, 1dc in 2dctog.
Round 4 1ch, 1sc in dc sp, [5ch, 1sc in next sp] 15 times, 5ch, ss in first sc. Fasten off.
Make 9 more motifs.

EDGING
Lay motifs out in a row. With RS facing, join thread in first sp of Row 3 of neckband.

Row 1 (RS) 1ch, 1sc in same sp as join, * [7ch, 1sc in next sp of neckband] 3 times, 3ch, 1sc in first sp of 1st motif, 3ch, 1sc in next sp of neckband, [1ch, 1sc in next sp of 1st motif, 1ch, 1sc in next sp of neckband] twice, 3ch, 1sc in next sp of 1st motif, 3ch, 1sc in next sp of neckband, [7ch, 1sc in next sp of neckband] 3 times **, 2ch, 1sc in next sp of neckband, rep from * 8 more times to join next 8 motifs, then rep from * to ** to join 10th motif, working 4ch, 1dc in last sp of neckband instead of last 7ch, 1sc in next sp.

Row 2 1ch, 1sc in first sp, 2ch, 2dctog in same sp, [1ch, 3dctog in next 7ch sp] twice, * 1ch, [3dctog in next 5ch sp, 7ch] 11 times, 3dctog in foll 5ch sp **, [1ch, 3dctog in next 7ch sp] 6 times, rep from * 8 more times, then rep from * to **, [1ch, 3dctog in 7ch sp] 3 times.

Row 3 * 3ch, ** 1sc in next 7ch sp, 3ch, [3dctog, 3ch] 3 times in foll 7ch sp, rep from ** 4 more times, 1sc in next 7ch sp, 3ch, 1sc in center 1ch sp, rep from * 9 more times, ending last rep 1sc in last 2dctog.

Row 4 3ch, *1dc in each of next 2 sps, [5ch, 1dc in next sp] twice, 5ch, rep from * 3 more times, 1dc in each of next 2 sps, ** 5ch, 1dc in foll sp, 5ch, 1dc in each of next 6 sps, 5ch, 1dc in next sp, 5ch, 1dc in each of next 2 sps, *** [5ch, 1tr in next sp] twice, 5ch, 1tr in each of next 2 sps, rep from *** two more times, then rep from ** 8 more times, [5ch, 1dc in next sp] 3 times, 1dc in foll sp, 3ch, 1sc in same sp as 3dctog. Fasten off.
Turn and join yarn at base of first picot at neck edge.

Row 5 1ch, [1sc, 5ch, ss in sc, 1sc] in each of first 4 sps, [1sc, 5ch, ss in sc, 1sc] twice in each 5ch sp, [1sc, 5ch, ss in sc, 1sc] in each of last 4 sps, ss in base of picot.
Fasten off.

TO FINISH

Darn in ends. Starch the collar, place RS down on a pressing board, pat into shape, pin out each picot, and press. Leave to dry before removing pins.

Love vintage? Get true Victorian style with this demure, delicate lace collar.

Fanciful Flower Earrings

It's easy to make crochet chain in soft color-coated copper wire. Curve the lengths of chain into petal shapes, glue them onto a base, and finish with a crystal stone for instant glamour in less than two hours.

ESTIMATED TIME TO COMPLETE

1½ hours for the pair

ABOUT THIS YARN

The 28-gauge (0.3-mm) colored copper wire used for the earrings is sold in 16-yd. (15-m) packs.

SIZE

Width 2 in. (5 cm)

YOU WILL NEED

- 1 x 16-yd. (15-m) pack of 28-gauge (0.3-mm) colored copper wire in deep pink
- C/2 (2.50-mm) crochet hook
- pair of round clip earring backs
- two crystal stones
- acrylic resin or epoxy resin adhesive

GAUGE

100 chain measures 2½ in. (6 cm) using C/2 (2.50-mm) hook. Change hook size if necessary to obtain this gauge.

ABBREVIATIONS

ch = chain

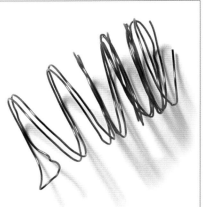

TIPS

- If your chain is a bit wiggly, push the round end of the hook into each chain to even them up. There's more wire in a pack than you'll need for one pair of earrings so there's plenty to experiment with.
- A pair of snipe-nose jewelry pliers is useful to flatten the petals, or lay the petals on a flat surface and tap gently with a small hammer. The wire becomes less flexible as you work, which helps to keep it in shape.
- Always take care when using acrylic resin adhesive. Open the back of the earring before you start, so the glue doesn't stick it together. Use a folded piece of cardboard or plastic to hold the earrings while the glue sets. Pliers or tweezers are useful for holding the petals while applying glue.

EARRINGS

Petals (Make 2) Make 100ch. Fasten off. Curve each chain length to form a six-petal flower, twisting starting and ending wires together, then through or around the chain to hold each petal in its shape. Twist the ends to secure and trim.

TO FINISH

Glue wire flower shapes onto earring backs, then glue on stones.

Create these delicate earrings with simple crochet cha

Pretty Pearly Necklace

All you need to know to make this necklace is how to work a crochet chain. The design is very adaptable—in fine thread with delicate beads, it looks very sophisticated; choose a thicker yarn with chunky beads for an ethnic effect.

ESTIMATED TIME TO COMPLETE
Each strand of beads 10 minutes, necklace 1 hour.

ABOUT THIS YARN
You can use any metallic sewing thread, but choose one that is strong enough to be used in a sewing machine so it won't break easily. The beads are coated glass, often sold as size 5 or 005.

SIZE
Length 22 in. (56 cm)

YOU WILL NEED
- 1 spool of metallic sewing thread in silver
- 500 small pearly beads
- B/1 (2.00-mm) crochet hook
- two hollow white metal beads
- necklace clasp

GAUGE
36 chain with 18 beads measures 4 in. (10 cm). Change hook size if necessary to obtain this gauge.

ABBREVIATIONS
ch = chain; [ ] = work instructions in brackets as directed.

NOTE
Leave long ends at each end of the strands so they can be used to attach the clasp.

TIP
Arrange 10 to 20 beads at a time tensioned on the thread between the middle finger of the left hand and the hook. Tilt the left hand forward each time to slide a bead close enough to catch with the left thumbnail; then make a chain.

This pretty necklace was made in just one hour.

NECKLACE
First strand Thread 100 beads on to the metallic sewing thread.
Make 2ch, [slide a bead up close to work, 2ch] 100 times. Fasten off.
Make 4 more strands in the same way.

TO FINISH
Knot strands together at one end. Twist strands loosely around each other and knot strands together at the other end. Slide a hollow bead on one end to cover the knot, and use the strand ends to attach one part of the clasp firmly, taking the ends back through the knot in the hollow bead before trimming. Attach the second part of the clasp to the other end of the necklace in the same way.

Crochet Beads

These beads are simply round balls of firm single crochet, filled with batting, so they are very quick and easy to make—each bead case can take just minutes to crochet. Using coral and turquoise evokes the natural colors of semiprecious stones, while the smooth cotton embroidery yarn gives a lovely iridescent sheen. You can also enjoy experimenting with different yarns, such as metallics, for a fun, contemporary effect, and mixing and matching colors and textures.

ESTIMATED TIME TO COMPLETE

For the shell of one bead 10 minutes, without stuffing and threading. For the necklace 2 hours; for the earrings about ½ hour.

ABOUT THIS YARN

The beads in the picture are worked in smooth mercerized 100 percent cotton perlé embroidery thread with 11 yd. (10 m) to a 5-g hank. See tips for alternative yarn suggestions.

SIZE

Each bead approximately ¾ in. (2 cm) across; **necklace length** (adjustable) 21½ in. (55 cm)

YOU WILL NEED

■ 1 x 5-g hank of embroidery thread in each of coral and turquoise
■ B/1 (2.00-mm) crochet hook
■ polyester fiberfill or batting
■ assorted ethnic white metal beads; 30 small round spacers; 14 medium beads and 7 large beads for the necklace; 4 small beads for the earrings
■ barrel catch; nylon cord; large sharp needle
■ 2 earring hooks; 2 small jump rings; jewelry pliers

GAUGE

16 sts measure 2⅜ in. (6 cm), 7 rows measure approx 1¼ in. (3 cm) over single crochet using B/1 (2.00-mm) hook. Change hook size if necessary to obtain this gauge.

ABBREVIATIONS

cont = continue; **dec** = decrease; **sc** = single crochet; **ss** = slip stitch; **st(s)** = stitch(es); [ ] = work instructions in brackets as directed.

TIPS

■ Wind the hank of embroidery yarn into a ball so it doesn't get tangled.
■ You can use any fine, firm yarn to make beads. Mercerized-cotton 4ply or metallic threads would also work well.
■ Adapt this design to suit yourself. Make a necklace using crochet beads alternated with small spacers; use a different shade of yarn for each pair of beads; make striped beads by changing color for each round. Create oval beads by working more rounds straight before the decrease round.
■ If you make a longer necklace, omit the catch and just join the ends at the back.
■ If you don't have jewelry pliers, you can use tweezers to attach the jump rings to the hooks.
■ Split jump rings are best for the earrings, but if you use ordinary rings don't pull the ends apart because this spoils the shape; always twist the ends in opposite directions, so that they'll line up neatly when you twist them back.

BEAD

Wind yarn around finger to make a ring.
Round 1 1ch, 8sc in ring, pull end to close ring, ss in first sc. 8 sts.

Round 2 1ch, [2sc in each sc] to end, ss in first sc. 16 sts.

Round 3 1ch, [1sc in each sc] to end, ss in first sc.

Round 3 forms sc. Cont in sc, work 3 more rounds.

Dec round 1ch, [miss 1sc, 1sc in next sc] 8 times, ss in first sc.

Leaving an end long enough to darn in, fasten off. Pack bead firmly with fiberfill or batting. Thread the thread end through the last round of sts, draw up, and secure. Darn the ends into the bead.

NECKLACE

Using coral, make four beads as given above, then make two larger beads by working one extra sc round before the dec round, and two smaller beads by working the dec round after the 3rd round.

TO FINISH

Lay the beads out with a metal bead in the center, spacer beads on each side, then the large crochet beads on either side. Alternate spacers, metal and crochet beads, ending with spacers and small metal beads at each side and at the back neck. Attach half of the barrel catch to the end of the cord. Using the sharp needle to push through the crochet beads, thread the beads on to the cord, attach the other half of the barrel catch and thread the ends of the cord back through the beads before trimming.

EARRINGS

Using turquoise and working into the back loop of each stitch to give a ridged effect, make two beads, leaving long thread ends.

TO FINISH

Close the top of each bead, thread the end down to the bottom, slip on a small bead, then bring the end back to the top. Thread on a second small bead, knot the thread through the jump ring, and secure the end in the bead. Attach the jump rings to earring hooks.

Jackets, Sweaters & Tops

Shaded-Blocks Sweater

Although the design of this clever sweater is based on a traditional granny square, the square is actually subtly shaped to make a flattering rectangle by working half-doubles instead of double crochet at each side on alternate rounds. The yarn is thick enough to work up quickly, yet it's soft and supple, so the sweater isn't heavy. The yoke, side panels, sleeves, and lower edging are all worked out from the blocks, so there's very little sewing required.

ESTIMATED TIME TO COMPLETE
For first size sweater, 18 hours.

ABOUT THIS YARN
Debbie Bliss Cashmerino Aran is a mix of 55 percent merino wool, 33 percent microfiber, and 12 percent cashmere. It has 98 yd. (90 m) to a 50-g ball.

SIZES
TO FIT: bust 34 to 36(**38 to 40**:42 to 44) in. [86 to 91(**96 to 102**:107 to 112) cm]
Actual measurements: bust 44(**47¼**:50½) in. [112(**120**:128) cm]; **length** 26⅜(**27⅛**:28) in. [67(**69**:71) cm]; **sleeve** 18 in. [46 cm].
Figures in parentheses refer to larger sizes. One figure refers to all sizes.

YOU WILL NEED
- 2(**3**:4) x 50-g balls of Debbie Bliss Cashmerino Aran, in navy, shade 207 (A)
- 8(**9**:10) x 50-g balls of same in blue, shade 208 (B)
- 3(**4**:4) x 50-g balls of same in pale blue, shade 202 (C)
- 2(**3**:3) x 50-g balls of same in cream, shade 101 (D)
- G/6 (4.50-mm) of crochet hook

GAUGE
Four rounds of block measure 3¾ x 4½ in. (9.5 x 11 cm); 17 rounds measure 17 x 20 in. (43 x 51 cm); 14 sts and 10 rows to 4 in. (10 cm) over half-double crochet, using G/6 (4.50-mm) hook. Change hook size if necessary to obtain this size block and gauge.

ABBREVIATIONS
ch = chain; **cont** = continue; **dc** = double crochet; **dec** - decrease; **foll** = following; **hdc** = half-double crochet; **2hdctog** = yarn around hook, insert hook in first st and pull loop through, yarn around hook, insert hook in next st and pull loop through, yarn around hook and pull through 5 loops on hook; **patt** = pattern; **rep** = repeat; **RS** = right side; **sc** = single crochet; **sp** = space; **ss** = slip stitch; **st(s)** = stitch(es); **WS** = wrong side; **[ ]** = work instructions in brackets as directed.

TIPS
■ To fasten off when working the squares, enlarge the last loop and pass the ball of yarn through. Where a color is used again after the next round, don't cut the yarn; just carry it up on the back of the work until needed.
■ You can save time at the end by darning in or working over the ends as you go.

BLOCK
Using A, wind yarn around finger to form a ring.
Round 1 (RS) 6ch, [3dc in ring, 3ch] 3 times, 2dc in ring, pull end to close ring, ss in 3rd ch. Fasten off.
Round 2 Join B in first sp, 5ch, 3dc in same sp as join, * 2ch, 3dc in next 3ch sp, 3ch, 3hdc in same 3ch sp, 2ch *, 3hdc in next 3ch sp, 3ch, 3dc in same sp, rep from * to *, 2hdc in first sp, ss in 2nd ch. Fasten off.
Round 3 Join C in first sp, 6ch, 3dc in same sp as join, 2ch, [3dc in next 2ch sp, 2ch, 3dc in next 3ch sp, 3ch, 3dc in same 3ch sp, 2ch] 3 times, 3dc in next 2ch sp, 2ch, 2dc in first sp, ss in 3rd ch. Fasten off.
Round 4 Join D in first sp, 5ch, 3dc in same sp as join, 2ch, * [3dc in next 2ch sp, 2ch] twice, 3dc in next 3ch sp, 3ch, 3hdc in same 3ch sp, 2ch, [3hdc in next 2ch sp, 2ch] twice *, 3hdc in next 3ch sp, 3ch, 3dc in same 3ch sp, 2ch, rep from * to *, 2hdc in first sp, ss in 2nd ch. Fasten off.
Cont as Rounds 3 and 4. Working one more group and space on each side each time, work

Turn two big blocks of
simple crochet into a
stunning sweater.

13 more rounds in color order: C, B, A, B, C, D, C, B, A, B, C, D, C. Fasten off.

BACK

Make block.

Yoke With RS facing you, placing joins in block at lower left and join B in top right corner sp.

Row 1 (RS) 3ch, 3dc in same sp as join, [3dc in each sp] to last sp, 4dc in last sp. 18 groups of sts. Change to A.

Row 2 1sc in first dc, 1ch, [1hdc in each dc] to last st, 1hdc in 3rd ch. 56 sts.

Row 3 1sc in first hdc, 1ch, [1hdc in each hdc] to last st, 1hdc in ch **.

Row 3 forms hdc. Cont in hdc, work 4 rows B, 1 row A. Fasten off.

FRONT

Work as given for back to **.

Shape neck Cont in B.

Next row (WS) 1sc in first hdc, 1ch, 1hdc in each of next 12 hdc, turn and complete right side on these 13 sts.

Cont in hdc, work 3 more rows B and 1 row A. Fasten off. With WS facing you, skip center 30 sts, join B in next st.

Next row 1sc in same place as join, 1ch, 1hdc in each hdc to last st, 1hdc in ch. 13 sts.

Complete in same way as right side.

RIGHT SIDE PANEL

Matching stitches, join shoulder seams. With RS facing you, join B in lower right back corner sp.

Row 1 (RS) 1sc in same place as join, 1ch, [1hdc in each of next 3dc, 1hdc in next sp] 17 times, 16hdc across row ends of yoke, 1hdc in corner sp of front, [1hdc in each of next 3dc, 1hdc in next sp] 17 times. 154 sts. Cont in hdc, work 3(**5**:7) more rows in B, 2 rows A, 1 row B.

Join sides With RS together and matching sts, insert hook through one st from each side together each time and work 52(**50**:48)sc. Fasten off.

LEFT SIDE PANEL

With RS facing you, join B in lower left front corner sp. Work as given for right side panel.

SLEEVES

With WS facing, join B at underarm.

Row 1 1sc in next st, 1ch, 1hdc in each of next 49(**53**:57) sts.

Cont in hdc and B on 50(**54**:58) sts, work two rows.

Dec row (RS) 1sc in first hdc, [1hdc in each hdc] to last 2 sts, 2hdctog. 48(**52**:56) sts.

Cont in hdc and A, dec in this way at each end of 7 foll 4th rows. 34(**38**:42) sts.

First size Work 1 row.

2nd size Dec one st at end of next row.

3rd size Dec one st at each end of next row.

All sizes 34(**37**:40) sts.

Border. Row 1 (RS) 1sc in first hdc, 2ch, 1dc in same hdc, [2ch, skip 2hdc, 3dc in next hdc] 10(**11**:12) times, 2ch, skip 2hdc, 2dc in last st. Fasten off.

With RS facing, join A in 2nd ch.

Row 2 (RS) 1sc in 2nd ch, 4ch, [3dc in next sp, 2ch] to end, 1dc in last dc. Fasten off. With RS facing, join B in first sp.

Row 3 [1sc, 2ch, 1dc] in first sp, [2ch, 3dc in next sp] to last sp, 2ch, 2dc in last sp.

Rows 2 and 3 form the border patt.

Joining yarn with RS facing each time, work 1 row in each of C, D, C, B, A, and B. Do not fasten off after last row, turn.

Edging row (WS) 1sc in first dc, 1ch, 1hdc in next dc, [1hdc in next sp, 1hdc in each of next 3dc] to last 2dc, 1hdc in last sp, 1hdc in each of last 2dc.

Fasten off. Darn in ends.

LOWER EDGING

With RS facing, join B in back right corner sp.

Round 1 1sc in same place as join, 1ch, 1hdc in each dc across back, 1hdc in corner sp, 16(**19**:22)hdc in row ends of right side panel, 1hdc in corner sp, 1hdc in each dc across front, 1hdc in corner sp, 16(**19**:22)hdc in row ends of left side panel, ss in ch, turn. 138(**144**:150) sts.

Round 2 1sc in same place as ss, 1ch, [1hdc in each hdc] to end, ss in ch, turn.

Turning each time, work 2(**4**:6) more rounds hdc.

Border. Round 1 (RS) 1sc in same place as ss, 4ch, [skip 2hdc, 3dc in next hdc, 2ch] to last 2 sts, 2dc in same place as sc, ss in 2nd ch.

Round 2 Ss in first sp, 1sc in first sp, 4ch, [3dc in next sp, 2ch] to end, 2dc in first sp, ss in 2nd ch.

Round 3 Ss in first sp, 1sc in first sp, 2ch, [3dc in next sp] to end, 2dc in first sp, ss in 2nd ch, turn.

Edging round (WS) 1sc in first dc, 1ch, [1hdc in each dc] to end, ss in ch.

Fasten off. Darn in ends.

COLLAR

With RS facing, join A in first st at right back neck.

Round 1 (RS) 1sc in same st as join, 1ch, 1hdc in each of next 29 hdc, change to B, 5hdc in row ends down left front neck, 1hdc in each of 30hdc across front neck, 5hdc in row ends up right front neck, ss in ch. 70 sts. Cont in hdc, work 10 more rounds in B. Fasten off. Darn in ends.

TO FINISH

Press according to ball band.

Join sleeve seams.

Sophisticated Silver Top

Pretty picots add interest to the simplest chain mesh fabric of this stunning yet easy-to-work top.

ESTIMATED TIME TO COMPLETE
For the 2nd-size top, 12 hours.

ABOUT THIS YARN
Rowan Lurex Shimmer is a lightweight, smooth, metallic-look yarn that's similar to a fingering-weight yarn. It's a mix of 80 percent viscose and 20 percent polyester with approximately 104 yd. (95 m) to a 25-g ball.

SIZES
TO FIT: bust 32(**34**:36:**38**) in. [81(**86**:91:**97**) cm]
ACTUAL MEASUREMENTS: bust 33(**36**:39½:**42½**) in. [84(**92**:100:**108**) cm]; **length** 20¾(**21½**:22¼:**23¼**) in. [53(**55**:56:**59**) cm]
Figures in parentheses refer to larger sizes. One figure refers to all sizes.

YOU WILL NEED
■ 5(**6**:7:**8**) × 25-g balls of Rowan Lurex Shimmer in Pewter, shade 333
■ No. 6 steel (1.75-mm) crochet hook

GAUGE
5 mesh spaces and 10 rows to 4 in. (10 cm) over picot mesh patt, when pressed, using No. 6 steel (1.75-mm) hook. Change hook size if necessary to obtain this gauge.

ABBREVIATIONS
ch = chain; **cont** = continue; **dec** = decrease; **patt** = pattern; **RS** = right side; **sc** = single crochet; **sp(s)** = space(s); **ss** = slip stitch; **tr** = triple; **WS** = wrong side; **[ ]** = work instructions in brackets as directed.

TIPS
■ This yarn is quite slippery, so keep a rubber band on the ball, releasing just enough yarn to work a single row at a time.
■ For extra control, wind the yarn one or two times around the middle finger of the left hand to add tension.
■ The fabric looks the same on both sides, but the edge stitches are different, so mark the right side of the work to make it easier to count the rows as you shape the armholes and neck.

BACK

Picot edging 3ch, 1sc in first ch, [4ch, 1sc in 3rd ch] 42(**46**:50:**54**) times. 43(**47**:51:**55**) picots.
Work into straight edge.
Row 1 (WS) 1ch, 1sc in first picot, [6ch, skip 1 picot, 1sc in next picot, 3ch, ss in sc] to last 2 picots, 6ch, 1sc in last picot.

21(**23**:25:**27**) mesh sps.
Row 2 7ch, 1sc in first 6ch sp, 3ch, ss in sc, [6ch, 1sc in next 6ch sp, 3ch, ss in sc] to end, 3ch, 1tr in sc of previous row.
Row 3 1ch, 1sc in tr, [6ch, 1sc in next 6ch sp, 3ch, ss in sc] to last 6ch sp, 6ch, 1sc in 4th ch.
Row 4 7ch, 1sc in first 6ch sp, 3ch, ss in sc,

[6ch, 1sc in next 6ch sp, 3ch, ss in sc] to end, 3ch, 1tr in sc.
Rows 3 and 4 form the picot mesh patt.
Cont in patt, work 30 more rows, ending with a 4th patt row.
Shape armholes. Row 1 1ch, 1sc in tr, 4ch, 1sc in first 6ch sp, [6ch, 1sc in next 6ch sp, 3ch, ss in sc] 18(**20**:22:**24**) times, 6ch, 1sc in next 6ch sp, 1tr in 4th ch, turn.
Dec row Ss in each of first 3ch, 1ch, 1sc in first sp, [6ch, 1sc in next 6ch sp, 3ch, ss in sc] 17(**19**:21:**23**) times, 6ch, 1sc in last 6ch sp.
Noting that instructions in brackets will be worked one less time on each row, work dec row 3 more times. 15(**17**:19:**21**) sps **.
Work 1 more dec row. 14(**16**:18:**20**) sps.
Starting next row with 7ch, patt 13(**15**:17:**19**) rows straight.
Finishing row 1ch, 1sc in tr, [4ch, 1sc in next sp] to last sp, 4ch, 1sc in 4th ch.

FRONT

Work as given for back to **.

Shape neck. Row 1 Ss in each of first
3ch, 1ch, 1sc in first sp, * [6ch, 1sc in
next 6ch sp, 3ch, ss in sc] 6(**7**:8:**9**) times,
6ch *, 1sc in center sp, rep from * to *, 6ch,
1sc in last sp.

Row 2 7ch, 1sc in first 6ch sp, [3ch, ss in sc,
6ch, 1sc in next 6ch sp] 5(**6**:7:**8**) times, 3ch,
ss in sc, 3ch, 1tr in 3rd ch, turn and
complete right side.

Row 3 6ch, 1sc in next 6ch sp, [3ch, ss in
sc, 6ch, 1sc in next 6ch sp] 4(**5**:6:**7**) times,
3ch, ss in sc, 6ch, 1sc in 3rd ch. 6(**7**:8:**9**) sps.
Noting that instructions in brackets will be
worked one time fewer on each row, work
Rows 2 and 3 three more times. 3(**4**:5:**6**) sps.

Next row 7ch, 1sc in first sp, [3ch, ss in sc,
6ch, 1sc in next sp] 2(**3**:4:**5**) times, 3ch, ss in
sc, 3ch, 1tr in 3rd ch.
Cont in patt, work 4(**6**:8:**10**) rows straight.
Work finishing row in same way as back.
With WS facing, join yarn in 6ch sp at left of
center for left side.

Row 1 6ch, [1sc in next 6ch sp, 3ch, ss in
sc, 6ch] 5(**6**:7:**8**) times, 3ch, ss in sc, 3ch,
1tr in tr.

Row 2 1ch, 1sc in tr, [6ch, 1sc in next 6ch
sp, 3ch, ss in sc] 5(**6**:7:**8**) times, 3ch, 1tr in
3rd ch.
Noting that instructions in brackets will be
worked one less time on each row, work
Rows 1 and 2 three more times. 3(**4**:5:**6**) sps.
Patt 5(**7**:9:**11**) rows straight.
Work finishing row in same way as back.

EDGING

Matching sts, join shoulders. Join yarn at
right shoulder and work a round of sc and
picots evenly around neck edge. Finish
armholes in the same way.

TO FINISH

Press according to ball band. Join side seams.

Layer this versatile
mesh top over a
skimpy camisole, a
slinky dress, or even
a slim-line sweater.

Cardigan with Lacy Edging

This gently fitted cardigan flatters the figure with its sophisticated style, while its simple stitch pattern combines single and double crochet. The openwork bands go quickly, along with the single crochet rows, which create tighter spacing. The pretty lacy edging looks complex but is actually worked in just three rows.

ESTIMATED TIME TO COMPLETE
For the first size cardigan, 25 hours.

ABOUT THIS YARN
Use any classic pure-wool 4ply or fingering yarn, with approximately 200 yd. (183 m) to a 50-g ball.

SIZES
To fit: bust 32–34(**36–38**:40–42:**44–46**) in. [81–86(**91–97**:102–107:**112–117**) cm]
Actual measurements: bust 35(**39½**:44:**48½**) in. [89(**100.5**:112:**123.5**) cm]; **length** 21½(**22**:23½:**24**) in. [55(**56**:60:**61**) cm]; **sleeve** 18½ in. [47 cm]
Figures in parentheses refer to larger sizes. One figure refers to all sizes.

YOU WILL NEED
- 7(**8**:9:**10**) x 50-g balls of pure-wool 4ply fingering yarn
- D/3 (3.00-mm) and C/2 (2.50-mm) crochet hooks

GAUGE
21 sts and 16 rows to 4 in. (10 cm) over patt, when pressed, using D/3 (3.00-mm) hook. Change hook size if necessary to obtain this gauge.

ABBREVIATIONS
beg = beginning; **ch** = chain; **cont** = continue; **dc** = double crochet; **2dctog** = leaving last loop of each stitch on the hook, work 2dc, yo and pull through 3 loops on hook; **3dctog** = leaving last loop of each stitch on the hook, work 3dc, yo and pull through 4 loops on hook; **dec** = decrease; **foll** = following; **inc** = increase; **patt** = pattern; **foll** = following; **RS** = right side; **sc** = single crochet; **sp(s)** = space(s); **ss** = slip stitch; **st(s)** = stitch(es); **3trcl** = leaving last loop of each stitch on the hook, work 3 triple sts, yo and pull through 4 loops on hook; **WS** = wrong side; **yo** = yarn over hook; [ ] = work instructions in brackets as directed.

NOTE
The fronts are two rows longer than the back, so that the pattern will match at the shoulders.

TIPS
- Use a larger hook to work the starting chain loosely and evenly, changing to a D/3 (3.00-mm) hook for the last 3ch to keep them neat.
- It's easy to see which side of the work you're on, because all wrong-side rows are in single crochet, while all right-side rows use double crochet stitches.
- You'll find it easy to keep track of the side and sleeve shaping if you mark each end of the decrease and increase rows.

Get in style with this simple, sexy cardigan.

BACK

Using D/3 (3.00-mm) hook, make 89(**101**:113:**125**)ch.

Row 1 (RS) 1dc in 4th ch from hook, [1dc in each ch] to end. 87(**99**:111:**123**) sts.

Row 2 1ch, [1sc in each dc] to last st, 1sc in top ch.

Row 3 1sc in first sc, 3ch, [skip 1sc, 1dc in next sc, 1ch] to end.

Row 4 1sc in first dc, [1sc in 1ch sp, 1sc in next dc] to end, working last sc in 2nd ch.

Row 5 1sc in first sc, 2ch, [1dc in each sc] to end.

Rows 2 to 5 form the patt.

Patt 3 more rows.

Dec row (RS) 1sc in first sc, 2ch, 3dctog, [1dc in each sc] to last 4 sc, 3dctog, 1dc in last sc. 83(**95**:107:**119**) sts.

Patt 3 rows, then work dec row again. 79(**91**:103:**115**) sts.

Patt 15 rows.

Inc row (RS) 1sc in first sc, 2ch, 3dc in next sc, 1dc in each sc to last 2 sc, 3dc in next sc, 1dc in last sc. 83(**95**:107:**119**) sts.

Cont in patt, inc in this way at each end of 2 foll 8th rows. 91(**103**:115:**127**) sts.

Patt 9(**9**:13:**13**) rows.

Shape armholes. Row 1 (RS) Ss in each of first 4(**4**:6:**6**) dc, [1sc, 3ch] in next sc, [skip 1sc, 1dc in next sc, 1ch] to last 4(**4**:6:**6**) sc, turn.

Row 2 1sc in first dc, [1sc in 1ch sp, 1sc in next st] to end. 83(**95**:103:**115**) sts.

Row 3 1sc in first sc, 2ch, 3dctog, 1dc in each sc to last 4 sc, 3dctog, 1dc in last sc.

Row 4 1ch, [1sc in each st] to end.

Row 5 [1sc, 2ch] in first sc, [skip 1sc, 1dc in next sc, 1ch] to last 4 sc, skip 1sc, placing first part dc in next sc and 2nd part dc in last sc, work 2dctog.

Row 6 1ch, 1sc in 2dctog, [1sc in next ch sp, 1sc in foll dc] to end.

Cont in patt, dec in same way as Rows 3 and 5 on next 1(**2**:3:**4**) RS rows. 71(**79**:83:**91**) sts.

Patt 25 rows. Fasten off.

LEFT FRONT

Using D/3 (3.00-mm) hook, make 43(**49**:55:**61**)ch.

Work Row 1 as given for back. 41(**47**:53:**59**) sts.

Work in patt as given for back for 7 more rows.

Dec row (RS) 1sc in first sc, 2ch, 3dctog, [1dc in each sc] to end. 39(**45**:51:**57**) sts.

Patt 3 rows then work dec row again. 37(**43**:49:**55**) sts.

Patt 15 rows.

Inc row (RS) 1sc in first sc, 2ch, 3dc in next sc, [1dc in each sc] to end. 39(**45**:51:**57**) sts.

Cont in patt, inc in this way at beg of 2 foll 8th rows. 43(**49**:55:**61**) sts.

Patt 9(**9**:13:**13**) rows.

Shape armhole and neck. Row 1 (RS) Ss in each of first 4(**4**:6:**6**)sc, [1sc, 3ch] in next sc, skip 1sc, 1dc in next sc, [1ch, skip 1sc, 1dc in next sc] to end. 39(**45**:49:**55**) sts.

Rows 2 to 6 Work as given for Rows 2 to 6 of back armhole shaping. 31(**37**:41:**47**) sts. Cont in patt, dec as set at each end of next 1(**2**:2:**2**) RS rows. 27(**29**:33:**39**) sts.

1st and 2nd sizes Cont in patt, dec in same way as before at end of 5 foll 4th rows.

3rd size Dec at beg of next RS row, at neck edge on foll RS row, then at neck edge on 4 foll 4th rows.

4th size Dec at beg of next RS row, at each end of foll RS row and at neck edge on 5 foll 4th rows.

All sizes 17(**19**:21:**23**) sts.

Patt 7(**7**:9:**7**) rows. Fasten off. Darn in ends.

RIGHT FRONT

Using D/3 (3.00-mm) hook, make 43(**49**:55:**61**)ch.

Work Row 1 as given for back. 41(**47**:53:**59**) sts.

Work in patt as given for back for 7 more rows.

Dec row (RS) 1sc in first sc, 2ch, [1dc in each sc] to last 4 sc, 3dctog, 1dc in last sc. 39(**45**:51:**57**) sts.

Patt 3 rows, then work dec row again. 37(**43**:49:**55**) sts.

Patt 15 rows.

Inc row (RS) 1sc in first sc, 2ch, 1dc in each sc to last 2 sc, 3dc in next sc, 1dc in last sc. 39(**45**:51:**57**) sts.

Cont in patt, inc in this way at end of 2 foll 8th rows. 43(**49**:51:**61**) sts.

Patt 9(**9**:13:**13**) rows.

Shape armhole and neck. Row 1 (RS) 1sc in first sc, 3ch, skip 1sc, 1dc in next sc, [1ch, skip 1sc, 1dc in next sc] to last 4(**4**:6:**6**) sc, turn. 39(**45**:49:**55**) sts.

Rows 2 to 6 Work as given for Rows 2 to 6 of back armhole shaping. 31(**37**:41:**47**) sts. Cont in patt, dec as set at each end of next 1(**2**:2:**2**) RS rows. 27(**29**:33:**39**) sts.

1st and 2nd sizes Cont in patt, dec in same way as before at beg of 5 foll 4th rows.

3rd size Dec at end of next RS row, at neck edge on foll RS row, then at neck edge on 4 foll 4th rows.

4th size Dec at end of next RS row, at each end of foll RS row and at neck edge on 5 foll 4th rows.

All sizes 17(**19**:21:**23**) sts.

Patt 7(**7**:9:**7**) rows. Fasten off. Darn in ends.

SLEEVES

Using D/3 (3.00-mm) hook, make 43(**47**:51:**55**)ch.

Work Row 1 as given for back. 41(**45**:49:**51**) sts.

Work 11 more rows in patt as given for back. Cont in patt, inc in same way as back at each end of next row and on 6(**6**:7:**7**) foll 8th rows. 69(**73**:81:**85**) sts.

Patt 13(**13**:5:**5**) rows.

Shape top Work as given for Rows 1 to 6 of back armhole shaping.

Cont in patt, dec in same way as Rows 3 and 5 of back on next 1(**2**:3:**4**) RS rows. 49 sts. Cont in patt, dec as before at each end of 3 foll 4th rows, then at each end of next 3 RS rows. 25 sts.

Work 1 row. Fasten off.

LACY EDGING

Matching sts, join shoulders.

Using C/2 (2.50-mm) hook and with RS facing, join yarn at lower edge of right front.

Row 1 (RS) Work 132(**136**:142:**146**)sc up right front edge, 34(**35**:41:**42**)sc across back neck and 132(**136**:142:**146**)sc down left front edge. 298(**307**:325:**334**) sts.

Row 2 1ch, 1sc in first sc, 4ch, skip 2sc, [1dc in next sc, 2ch, skip 2sc] to last sc, 1dc in last sc.

Row 3 [6ch, 1dc in first ch, skip first sp, 3trcl in next sp, 6ch, 1dc in first ch, 3trcl in same sp, 6ch, 1dc in next ch, skip next sp, 1sc in next dc] 33(**34**:36:**37**) times.

Fasten off. Darn in ends.

CUFF EDGINGS

Using C/2 (2.50-mm) hook and with WS facing, join yarn and work 1sc in each starting ch. 41(**45**:49:**53**) sts.

Picot row (RS) 1sc in first sc, [6ch, ss in first ch, 1sc in each of next 2sc] to end. Fasten off. Darn in ends.

TO FINISH

Press lightly. Join side and sleeve seams. Set in sleeves. Finish lower edge of cardigan in same way as cuffs. Make a 24 in. (61 cm) length of chain. Fasten off. Slip through lace edging and tie.

Silk Sampler Jacket

The bands of lacy pattern may look complex, but they're made with just the basic crochet stitches. Because the jacket is made in one piece to the armholes, the patterns match all the way around. By the time you shape the neck, you're familiar with the patterns, so you'll have an instinctive feel for where the patterns break, and the sleeves are the simplest mesh.

ESTIMATED TIME TO COMPLETE
For the first size, 20 hours.

ABOUT THIS YARN
Debbie Bliss Pure Silk is a single-twist 100 percent silk yarn with occasional slubs. It has approximately 136 yd (125 m). to a 50-g ball.

SIZES
TO FIT: bust 32 to 34(**36 to 38**:40 to 42) in. [81 to 86(**91 to 97**:102 to 107) cm]
ACTUAL MEASUREMENTS: bust 37(**41½**:46) in. [94(**105.5**:117) cm]; **length** 26(**26¾**:28) in. [66(**68**:71) cm]; **sleeve** 18 in. [46 cm]
Figures in parentheses refer to larger sizes. One figure refers to all sizes.

YOU WILL NEED
- 9(**11**:13) x 50-g balls of Debbie Bliss Pure Silk in turquoise, shade 07
- G/6 (4.50-mm) crochet hook

GAUGE
21 sts to 4 in. (10 cm) over single crochet, 6 rows of shell patt measure 3½ in. (9 cm), 6 rows of mesh patt measure 2¾ in. (7 cm), 8 rows of fan patt measure 2¾ in. (7 cm), all when pressed using G/6 (4.50-mm) hook. Change hook size if necessary to obtain these gauges.

ABBREVIATIONS
beg = beginning; **ch** = chain; **cont** = continue; **dc** = double; **2dctog** = leaving last loop of each st on hook, work 2dc, yo and pull through 3 loops on hook; **patt** = pattern; **rep** = repeat; **sc** = single crochet; **2sctog** = insert hook in first st and pull loop through, insert hook in next st and pull loop through, yo and pull through 3 loops on hook; **sp** = space; **ss** = slip stitch; **st(s)** = stitch(es); **tr** = triple; **yo** = yarn over hook; **[ ]** = work instructions in brackets as directed.

NOTE
The jacket is worked in one piece to the armholes, then divided for the fronts and the back.

TIPS
■ The chain stitches, especially when working the mesh pattern, should be neat but not too tight. If you work tightly, you may need to add an extra chain to create a flexible fabric.
■ If you'd like to make a matching covered button from leftover yarn, you'll need a smooth domed button or a button mold and a C/2 (2.50-mm) crochet hook. Wind yarn around finger to form a ring, work 8sc in ring, then continue in a spiral working 2sc in each sc until cover is almost the same size as the button, work a few rounds without increasing, then skip alternate sc until cover fits over button. Insert button and work 2sctog in remaining sc until gap is as small as possible. Fasten off, thread end of yarn through stitches, draw up, and secure.

BACK AND FRONTS
Scallop edging. Row 1 [Make 10ch, ss in first ch to form a ring, 9sc in ring] 32(**36**:40) times, turn.
Row 2 1ch, [1sc in each sc] to end, do not turn. Work in patt along top edge.
Row 1 (RS) 1ch, 1sc in row end of first sc, [5sc in sp, 1sc between scallops] 31(**35**:39) times, 5sc in last sp, 1sc in row end of last sc. 193(**217**:241) sts.
Row 2 1ch, [1sc in each sc] to end.
This row forms sc. Work 1 more row sc.
Row 4 1ch, 1sc in first sc, 2ch, * skip 2sc, [3dc, 1ch, 3dc] in next sc, skip 2sc, 1dc in next sc, rep from * 31(**35**:39) more times.

This sophisticated jacket
is easier than it looks.

Row 5 1sc in first dc, 4ch, [1sc in 1ch sp, 2ch, skip 3dc, 1dc in next dc, 2ch] to end, omitting last 2ch and working last dc in 2nd ch.

Row 6 1sc in first dc, 2ch, 3dc in same dc as sc, [1dc in next sc, 3dc in next dc, 1ch, 3dc in same dc] to last dc, 1dc in last sc, 4dc in 2nd ch.

Row 7 1sc in first dc, [2ch, skip 3dc, 1dc in next dc, 2ch, 1sc in 1ch sp] to end, working last sc in 2nd ch.

Row 8 1sc in first sc, 2ch, * [3dc, 1ch, 3dc] in next dc, 1dc in next sc, rep from * to end.

Row 9 As Row 5.

Rows 4 to 9 form shell patt.

Row 10 1ch, 1sc in first dc, [2sc in 2ch sp, 1sc in sc, 2sc in 2ch sp, 1sc in dc] to end, working last sc in 2nd ch. 193(**217**:241) sts. Work 1 row sc.

Row 12 1ch, 1sc in first sc, [6ch, skip 2sc, 1sc in next sc] to end.

Row 13 5ch, 1sc in first 6ch sp, [2ch, 1sc in next 6ch sp] to last sp, 2ch, 1dc in sc.

Row 14 1ch, 1sc in dc, 6ch, skip first 2ch sp, [1sc in next 2ch sp, 6ch] to end, 1sc in 3rd ch.

Rows 15, 16, and 17 As Rows 13, 14, and 13.

Rows 12 to 17 form mesh patt.

Row 18 1ch, 1sc in dc, 1sc in first 2ch sp, [1sc in next sc, 2sc in next 2ch sp] to last 2ch sp, 1sc in last sc, 1sc in 5ch sp, 1sc in 3rd ch. 193(**217**:241) sts.

Row 19 1ch, [1sc in each sc] to end.

Row 20 1ch, 1sc in first sc, * 2ch, skip 2sc, 1sc in next sc, 1ch, skip 2sc, [2dctog, 1ch] 3 times in next sc, skip 2sc, 1sc in next sc, 2ch, skip 2sc, 1sc in next sc, rep from * to end.

Row 21 1ch, 1sc in first sc, 1ch, * 1sc in next 2ch sp, 1ch, [2dctog in next 1ch sp, 1ch] 4 times, 1sc in next 2ch sp, 1ch, rep from * to end, omitting last ch.

Row 22 1ch, 1sc in first sc, 8ch, [1sc in 1ch sp between center pair of 2dctog, 5ch, 1tr in 1ch sp between 2sc, 5ch] to end, omitting last 5ch and working last tr in last sc.

Row 23 1ch, 1sc in tr, [5sc in next 5ch sp, 1sc in sc, 5sc in foll 5ch sp, 1sc in tr] to end. 193(**217**:241) sts.

Rows 24, 25, 26, 27, 28, and 29 As Rows 19, 20, 21, 22, 23, and 19. 193(**217**:241) sts.

Rows 20 to 27 form fan patt.

Work Rows 12 to 19, then Rows 4 to 11 again.

Left front. Row 1 (WS) 1ch, 1sc in first sc, [6ch, skip 2sc, 1sc in next sc] 14(**16**:18) times, turn.

Row 2 5ch, 1sc in first ch sp, [2ch, 1sc in next ch sp] 13(**15**:17) times.

Row 3 1ch, 1sc in first sp, [6ch, 1sc in next sp] 12(**14**:16) times, 6ch, 1sc in 3rd ch.

Row 4 5ch, 1sc in first sp, [2ch, 1sc in next sp] 12(**14**:16) times.

Row 5 1ch, 1sc in first sp, [6ch, 1sc in next sp] 11(**13**:15) times, 6ch, 1sc in 3rd ch.

Row 6 5ch, 1sc in first sp, [2ch, 1sc in next sp] 11(**13**:15) times.

Row 7 1ch, 2sc in first sp, [1sc in next sc, 2sc in next sp] 10(**12**:14) times, 1sc in next sc, 1sc in last sp, 1sc in 3rd ch.

Row 8 1ch, 1sc in each sc to last 2sc, 2sctog. 34(**40**:46) sts.

Row 9 1ch, [skip 1sc, 1sc in next sc] twice, * 2ch, skip 2sc, 1sc in next sc, 1ch, skip 2sc, [2dctog, 1ch] 3 times in next sc, skip 2sc, 1sc in next sc, 2ch, skip 2sc, 1sc in next sc, rep from * 1(2:2) times, **1st and 3rd sizes** 2ch, skip 2sc, 1sc in next sc, 1ch, skip 2sc, [2dctog, 1ch, 2dctog] in last sc.

Row 10. 1st and 3rd sizes 1sc in first 2dctog, 3ch, [2dctog in next 1ch sp, 1ch] twice, **all sizes** patt as Row 21 until sc in last 2ch sp has been completed, 1ch, 1sc in sc, ss in last sc.

Row 11 1ch, 1sc in first 1ch sp, 6ch, 1sc in 1ch sp between center pair of 2dctog, patt as Row 22, **1st and 3rd sizes** ending 1sc in 2nd ch.

Row 12. 1st and 3rd sizes 1ch, 1sc in first sc, **all sizes** work Row 23 to last sc in 1ch sp, 3ch, 3sc in 6ch sp. 28(**34**:40) sts.

Row 13 1ch, skip first sc, [1sc in each sc] to end. 27(**33**:39) sts.

Row 14. 1st and 3rd sizes 3ch, [2dctog, 1ch] twice in first sc, **all sizes** patt as Row 20 until 2nd 2dctog of last motif has been completed, 1tr in last sc.

Row 15 1ch, 1sc in first 2dctog, 4ch, [2dctog in next 1ch sp, 1ch] twice, patt as Row 21, **1st and 3rd sizes** ending 1dc in last 2dctog.

Row 16. 1st and 3rd sizes 1ch, 1sc in first 1ch sp, **all sizes** patt as Row 22 until last tr in 1ch sp is complete, 4ch, sc in 4ch sp.

Row 17 1ch, skip first sc, 4sc in 4ch sp, patt as Row 23 to end.

Row 18 1ch, [1sc in each sc] to last 2sc, 2sctog. 22(**28**:34) sts.

Beg with Row 12, cont in patt, work 6(**8**:10) rows, then work Rows 17, 18, and 19. Fasten off.

Back With WS facing, leave 11sc for left armhole, join yarn in next st.

Row 1 1ch, 1sc in same place as join, [6ch, skip 2sc, 1sc in next sc] 28(**32**:36) times, turn.

Cont in patt until back matches front to shoulder, **1st and 3rd sizes** Working half repeats at ends of rows where necessary in same way as given for left front. Fasten off.

Right front With WS facing, leave 11sc of right armhole, join yarn in next st.

Row 1 1ch, 1sc in same place as join, [6ch, skip 2sc, 1sc in next sc] 13(**15**:17) times, 3ch, skip 2sc, 1dc in last sc.

Row 2 1sc in first sp, [2ch, 1sc in next sp] to end, 1ch, 1dc in last sc.

Beg and ending in this way, patt 4 more rows.

Row 7 1sc in dc, skip 1ch sp, [1sc in next sc, 2sc in next 2ch sp] to end, 1sc in last sc. 35(**41**:47) sts.

Row 8 1ch, skip first sc, [1sc in each sc] to end. 34(**40**:46) sts.

Row 9. 1st and 3rd sizes 3ch, [2dctog, 1ch] twice in first sc, **all sizes** patt as Row 20 until last group of 2dctog, 1ch has been completed, skip 2sc, 1sc in next sc, 2ch, skip 2sc, 1sc in next sc, 1ch, skip 1sc, 1sc in foll sc.

Row 10 1ch, 1sc in 1ch sp, 1ch, 1sc in next sp, patt as Row 21, **1st and 3rd sizes** ending 1dc in last 2dctog.

Row 11. 1st and 3rd sizes 1ch, 1sc in dc, **all sizes** patt as Row 22 until last sc in center sp of last group of 2dctog, has been completed, 3ch, 1tr in last sc.

Row 12 1ch, skip tr, 3sc in 3ch sp, patt as Row 23, **1st and 3rd sizes** ending 1sc in last sc. 28(**34**:40) sts.

Row 13 1ch, [1sc in each sc] to last 2sc, 2sctog. 27(**33**:39) sts.

Row 14 Ss in first sc, 4ch, skip 2sc, [2dctog, 1ch] twice in next sc, patt as Row 20, **1st and 3rd sizes** ending [1ch, 2dctog] twice in last sc, 1dc in last sc.

Row 15. 1st and 3rd sizes 1sc in first

2dctog, 3ch, **all sizes** patt as Row 21 until 2nd 2dctog, 1ch of last motif have been completed, 1tr in 4th ch.

Row 16 1sc in tr, 4ch, patt as Row 22, **1st and 3rd sizes** ending 1sc in 3ch sp.

Row 17 Patt as Row 23 until sc in last tr is complete, 3sc in last 4ch sp, 1sc in last sc.

Row 18 1ch, [1sc in each sc] to last 2sc, 2sctog. 22(**28**:34) sts.

Complete to match left front.

SLEEVES

Matching sts, join shoulders. With RS facing, work 94(**103**:112) sc evenly along row ends of armhole edge. Repeating Rows 12 and 13 to form mesh patt, work in mesh patt for 6 rows.

Shape sleeve. Row 1 1sc in first sc, [6ch, 1sc in next 2ch sp] to last 2ch sp, 3ch, 1dc in 3rd ch.

Row 2 1ch, 1sc in first sp, [2ch, 1sc in next 6ch sp] to last 6ch sp.

Row 3 1ch, 1sc in first sp, [6ch, 1sc in next 2ch sp] until one 2ch sp remains, [yo] twice, insert hook in last 2ch sp, then in last sc, [yo, pull through] 3 times.

Work last 2 rows 5(**6**:7) more times.

Next row 1ch, 1sc in first sp, [6ch, 1sc in next sp] to end, 1sc in last sc.

Cont in patt, work 22(**20**:18) more rows.

2nd size Decreasing 3 sts evenly across row, **all sizes** work 1 row sc in same way as Row 15 of back and fronts. 52(**52**:58) sts.

Edging. Row 1 1sc in each of first 3sc, [5ch, skip 3sc, 1sc in each of next 3sc] to end, 1sc in last sc.

Row 2 1ch, skip first sc, ss in next sc, skip 1sc, [9sc in 5ch sp, skip 1sc, ss in next sc, skip 1sc] to end, ss in last sc.

Row 3 Skip first sc, [1sc in each of next 9 sc, 1sc in sc with ss of 2nd row] to end, ending ss in last sc. Fasten off. Darn in ends.

FRONT EDGING

With RS facing, work 262(**274**:286)sc evenly up right front edge, around neck and down left front edge. Work edging as given for sleeves.

TO FINISH

Press according to ball band. Join row ends at top of sleeves to 11 sts left at underarms and join sleeve seams. Join ends of edgings. Darn in ends.

Aran-Style Coat

The stitch pattern of this slightly flared three-quarter-length coat couldn't be simpler—it's just alternate rows of double and single crochet. Double crochet rows make it grow quickly, while the single crochet adds stability to the fabric. The Aran-effect pattern of raised lines and bobbles is made by working surface-chain diamonds and bobbles, so you can add more decoration to your coat or just leave it plain.

ESTIMATED TIME TO COMPLETE
For the 2nd-size coat, 28 hours.

ABOUT THIS YARN
Debbie Bliss Merino Aran is a beautifully soft, smooth 100 percent merino-wool yarn with 85 yd. (78 m) to a 50-g ball.

SIZES
To fit: bust 32(**34**:36:**38**:40:**42**:44:**46**) in.
[81(**86**:91:**97**:102:**107**:112:**117**) cm]
Actual measurements: bust 34(**36¼**:38½:**40¾**:43:**45¼**:47½:**49¾**) in.
[86.5(**92.5**:98:**103.5**:109.5:**115**:121:**126.5**) cm];
length 30½(**31½**:31½:**32¼**:33:**33¼**:34:**35**) in. [77.5(**80**:80:**82**:84.5:**86.5**:86.5:**89**) cm];
sleeve 19¼ in. [49 cm].
Figures in parentheses refer to larger sizes. One figure refers to all sizes.

YOU WILL NEED
- 20(**21**:22:**23**:24:**25**:26:**27**) x 50-g balls of Debbie Bliss Merino Aran, in shade 101
- H/8 (5.00-mm) and J/10 (6.00-mm) crochet hooks
- 5 buttons

GAUGE
14 sts and 9 rows to 4 in. (10 cm) over double and single crochet pattern, when pressed, using J/10 (6.00-mm) hook. Change hook size if necessary to obtain this gauge.

ABBREVIATIONS
beg = beginning; **ch** = chain; **cont** = continue; **dc** = double crochet; **2dctog** = leaving last loop of each st on hook, work 2dc, yo and pull through 3 loops on hook; **dec** = decrease; **foll** = following; **inc** = increase; **patt** = pattern; **RS** = right side; **sc** = single crochet; **2sctog** = insert hook in next st, yo and pull through, insert hook in foll st, yo and pull through, yo and pull through 3 loops on hook; **ss** = slip stitch; **sp** = space; **st(s)** = stitch(es); **WS** = wrong side; **yo** = yarn over hook; **[ ]** = work instructions in brackets as directed.

BACK
Ribbing Using H/8 (5.00-mm) hook, make 13ch.
Row 1 (RS) 1dc in 4th ch from hook, [1dc in each ch] to end. 11 sts.
Row 2 1ch, skip first dc, [1sc around stem of each st] to end. 10 sts.
Row 3 3ch, [1dc in each sc] to end. 11 sts.
Rows 2 and 3 form the ribbing patt.
Work 68(**72**:76:**80**:84:**88**:92:**96**) more rows, ending with a Row 3.
Do not fasten off; turn and work along row ends.
Edging. Row 1 (RS) 1ch, 2sc in first dc, [1sc in next ridge, 1sc in next dc] to end, 1sc in end ch.
Row 2 1ch, [1sc around stem of each sc] to end, 1sc around end ch.
74(**78**:82:**86**:90:**94**:98:**102**) sts.
Change to J/10 (6.00-mm) hook.
Row 1 (RS) 1sc in first sc, 2ch, [1dc in each sc] to end.
Row 2 1ch, [1sc in each dc] to end, 1sc in 2nd ch.

These 2 rows form the dc and sc patt.

Dec row (RS) 1sc in first sc, 2ch, 1dc in next sc, 2dctog, [1dc in each sc] to last 4sc, 2dctog, 1dc in each of last 2sc.

Cont in dc and sc patt, dec in this way at each end of 7 foll 4th rows.
58(**62**:66:**70**:74:**78**:82:**86**) sts.

Patt 13(**13**:13:**13**:15:**15**:15:**15**) rows.

Shape armholes. Next row (RS) Ss in each of first 2(**3**:3:**4**:4:**5**:5:**6**)sc, 1sc in next sc, 2ch, [1dc in each sc] to last 2(**3**:3:**4**:4:**5**:5:**6**)sc, turn.
54(**56**:60:**62**:66:**68**:72:**74**) sts.

Cont in dc and sc patt, dec in same way as before at each end of next 2(**2**:3:**3**:4:**4**:5:**5**) RS rows. 50(**52**:54:**56**:58:**60**:62:**64**) sts.

Patt 13(**15**:13:**15**:13:**15**:13:**15**) rows.
Fasten off. Darn in ends.

LEFT FRONT

Ribbing Work as given for back ribbing until 35(**37**:39:**41**:43:**45**:47:**49**) rows have been completed.

Work 1st and 2nd edging rows as given for back. 38(**40**:42:**44**:46:**48**:50:**52**) sts.

Change to J/10 (6.00-mm) hook.

Work 2 rows in dc and sc patt as given for back **.

Dec row (RS) 1sc in first sc, 2ch, 1dc in next sc, 2dctog, [1dc in each sc] to end.

Cont in dc and sc patt, dec in this way at beg of 7 foll 4th rows.
30(**32**:34:**36**:38:**40**:42:**44**) sts.

Patt 13(**13**:13:**13**:15:**15**:15:**15**) rows.

Shape armhole. Next row (RS) Ss in each of first 2(**3**:3:**4**:4:**5**:5:**6**)sc, 1sc in next sc, 2ch, [1dc in each sc] to end.
28(**29**:31:**32**:34:**35**:37:**38**) sts.

Cont in dc and sc patt, dec in same way as before at beg of next 2(**2**:3:**3**:4:**4**:5:**5**) RS rows. 26(**27**:28:**29**:30:**31**:32:**33**) sts.

Get an Aran look the easy way with this stylish coat.

■ The coat shown here has panels of decoration only on the front; the back of the jacket is plain. If you prefer a more detailed design, you could add more lines of bobbles to each of the front panels or work panels on the back and the sleeves, too. Remember that if you do, you may need some additional yarn.

■ If, on the other hand, you decide not to work the decorative panels on your coat at all, you may be able to get away with one less ball of yarn.

■ Working around the stem of a stitch tips the chain edge to the right side, giving a rib effect. Simply insert the hook from right to left, in and out again behind the stem at the top of the double to work the sc stitch.

■ When working the surface bobbles, you may find it easier to bring your left hand on top to work the 5ch.

■ It's easy to see which side of the work you're on, because all RS rows are dc rows.

■ All side and sleeve shapings are made on RS rows. Mark the shaping rows to help keep count of how many pairs of increases or decreases you've worked.

Patt 5(**7**:5:**7**:5:**7**:5:**7**) rows.

Shape neck. Row 1 (RS) 1sc in first sc, 2ch, 1dc in each of next 12(**13**:14:**15**:15:**16**:17:**18**)sc, 2dctog, 1dc in each of next 2 sc, turn and leave 9(**9**:9:**9**:10:**10**:10:**10**)sc free for neck. 16(**17**:18:**19**:19:**20**:21:**22**) sts.

Row 2 1ch, 2sctog, 1sc in each st to end.

Row 3 1sc in first sc, 2ch, 1dc in each sc to last 4sc, 2dctog, 1dc in each of last 2sc.

Row 4 As Row 2.

13(**14**:15:**16**:16:**17**:18:**19**) sts.

Patt 4 rows. Fasten off. Darn in ends.

RIGHT FRONT

Work as given for left front to **.

Dec row (RS) 1sc in first sc, 2ch, [1dc in each sc] to last 4sc, 2dctog, 1dc in each of last 2sc.

Cont in dc and sc patt, dec in this way at end of 7 foll 4th rows. 30(**32**:34:**36**:38:**40**:42:**44**) sts.

Patt 13(**13**:13:**13**:15:**15**:15:**15**) rows.

Shape armhole. Next row (RS) 1sc in first sc, 2ch, [1dc in each sc] to last 2(**3**:3:**4**:4:**5**:5:**6**)sc, turn. 28(**29**:31:**32**:34:

35:**37**:38) sts.Cont in dc and sc patt, dec in same way as before at end of next 2(**2**:3:**3**:4:**4**:5:**5**) RS rows. 26(**27**:28:**29**:30:**31**:32:**33**) sts.Patt 5(**7**:5:**7**:5:**7**:5:**7**) rows. Fasten off.

Shape neck. Row 1 (RS) Join yarn in 10th(**10th**:10th:**10th**:11th:**11th**:11th:**11th**) sc from front edge, 1sc in same sc, 2ch, 1dc in next sc, 2dctog, [1dc in each sc] to end. 16(**17**:18:**19**:19:**20**:21:**22**) sts.

Row 2 1ch, [1sc in each st] to last 2 sts, 2sctog.

Row 3 1sc in first sc, 2ch, 1dc in next sc, 2dctog, [1dc in each sc] to end.
Row 4 As Row 2.
13(**14**:15:**16**:16:**17**:18:**19**) sts.
Patt 4 rows. Fasten off.

SLEEVES

Ribbing Work as given for back ribbing until 27(**29**:29:**31**:31:**33**:33:**35**) rows have been completed.
Work first and 2nd edging rows as given for back. 30(**32**:32:**34**:34:**36**:36:**38**) sts.
Change to J/10 (6.00-mm) hook. Work 6(**4**:4:**2**:2:**2**:2:**2**) rows in dc and sc patt as given for back.

Inc row (RS) 1sc in first sc, 2ch, 1dc in next sc, 2dc in foll sc, [1dc in each sc] to last 3sc, 2dc in next sc, 1dc in each of last 2sc. Cont in dc and sc patt, inc in this way at each end of 3(**4**:4:**3**:3:**0**:0:**0**) foll 6th rows, 2(**1**:1:**3**:3:**8**:8:**7**) foll 4th rows and next 0(**1**:1:**1**:1:**0**:0:**2**) RS rows.
42(**46**:46:**50**:50:**54**:54:**58**) sts. Patt 3(**1**:1:**1**:1:**1**:1:**1**) rows.

Shape top. Next row (RS) Ss in each of first 2(**3**:3:**4**:4:**5**:5:**6**)sc, 1sc in next sc, 2ch, [1dc in each sc] to last 2(**3**:3:**4**:4:**5**:5:**6**)sc, turn. 38(**40**:40:**42**:42:**44**:44:**46**) sts.
Cont in dc and sc patt, dec in same way as back at each end of next 1(**2**:2:**3**:3:**4**:4:**5**) RS rows. 36 sts.
2nd dec row (WS) 2sctog, [1sc in each dc] to last 2 sts, 2sctog. 34 sts.
3rd dec row (RS) 1sc in first st, 2ch, 1dc in next sc, [2dctog] twice, [1dc in each sc] to last 6 sts, [2dctog] twice, 1dc in each of last 2 sts. 30 sts.
Work 2nd and 3rd dec rows once more, then work 2nd dec row again. 22 sts.
Fasten off. Darn in ends.

FRONT BANDS

Left front Using H/8 (5.00-mm) hook, join yarn at neck edge.
Row 1 Work 95(**98**:98:**101**:104:**107**:107:**110**)sc along front edge.
Row 2 1ch, skip first sc, [1sc around stem of each sc] to end.
94(**97**:97:**100**:103:**106**:106:**109**) sts.
Row 3 1ch, [1sc in each sc] to end **.
Row 3 forms sc. Work 2 more rows sc. Do not turn after last row.
Work 1 row crab st (sc backward).
Fasten off. Darn in ends.
Right front Joining yarn at lower edge, work as given for left front band to **.
Buttonhole row (WS) 1ch, 1sc in each of first 2sc, [2ch, skip 2sc, 1sc in each of next 13(**13**:13:**14**:14:**15**:15:**15**) sc] 4 times, 2ch, skip 2sc, [1sc in each sc] to end.
Next row 1ch, [1sc in each sc and 2sc in each 2ch sp] to end. Do not fasten off. Work 1 row crab st (sc backward).
Fasten off. Darn in ends.

COLLAR

Matching sts, join shoulders. Using H/8 (5.00-mm) hook, join yarn in ridge at beg of right front band.
Row 1 Work 23(**23**:23:**23**:24:**24**:24:**24**)sc up right front neck, 24(**24**:24:**24**:26:**26**:26:**26**)sc across back neck and 23(**23**:23:**23**:24:**24**:24:**24**)sc down left front neck ending with last sc in ridge at beg of left front band. 70(**70**:70:**70**:74:**74**:74:**74**) sc.
Row 2 1ch, [1sc in each sc] to end.
Row 2 forms sc. Change to J/10 (6.00-mm) hook. Work 18 more rows sc. Fasten off.
Edging Using H/8 (5.00-mm) hook, join yarn in corner of right front band and work 1 row of crab st (sc backward) along row ends of band, row ends of collar, in sc along edge, down row ends of collar and along row ends of band. Fasten off. Darn in all ends.

TO FINISH

Press according to ball band. Set in sleeves. Add surface decoration. Join side and sleeve seams. Sew on buttons.

SURFACE DECORATION

Diamond panel 1. First line Using J/10 (6.00-mm) hook and with RS facing, start above welt in 2nd edging row on right front. Holding yarn underneath front, insert hook between dc and band edging and bring a loop of yarn to RS. Work 1ch over lower part of first dc to the left, 1ch over upper part of foll dc to the left, 3rd ch in sp after next sc in row above to the left, 4th ch in sp next to dc in row above sc, 5th ch over lower part of dc in row above to the right, 6th ch over upper part of foll dc to the right, 7th ch in sp after next sc in row above to the right and 8th ch in sp between dc in row above sc. Cont in this way working 4 surface ch left and 4 right until neck edge. Fasten off.
2nd line Placing surface chain so that chains share the same hole when they meet and working from right to left, then left to right, work 2nd line in the same way. Placing pairs of lines so that there are 3dc between widest part of diamonds, work 2 more panels on right front, then work 3 panels on left front.
Surface bobbles Worked up center diamond panel on each front. Using J/10 (6.00-mm) hook, with RS facing you and the yarn underneath, join yarn and bring a loop through to one side of sc in center of first outlined area at lower edge. * Work 5ch, take hook to the other side of sc, bring loop up and pull through last ch, lengthen ch and remove hook, insert hook to one side where surface ch of diamonds meet above, bring hook out by loop and tensioning loop so fabric lies flat, pull long ch through on back of work, work 1ch over surface ch at point of diamond, pull up loop and remove hook, insert hook in center of next outlined area, bring hook out by loop and pull long ch through on back of work. Rep from * until all diamonds in the panel have a center 5ch bobble. Fasten off. Darn in all ends.

Frilly-Edged Sweater

Let the yarn do the work! This shapely scoop-neck sweater is worked almost completely in single crochet, with longer stitches for the ruffle at the lower edge, the neckline, and around the three-quarter-length sleeves.

ESTIMATED TIME TO COMPLETE

For the 2nd-size sweater, 24 hours.

ABOUT THIS YARN

Sirdar Medici is a lightweight yarn that combines a bouclé core with bright highlight fiber. It's a mix of 70 percent nylon, 28 percent cotton, and 2 percent polyester and has approximately 104 yd. (95 m) to a 50-g ball.

SIZES

To fit: bust 32(**34**:36:**38**:40) in. [81(**86**:91:**97**:102) cm]

Actual measurements: bust 33½(**36**:39½:**41¼**:43¾) in. [85(**91.5**:98:**105**:111.5) cm]; **length** 22¼(**22¾**:23¼:**24**:24½) in. [56.5(**58**:59.5:**61**:62.5) cm]; **sleeve** 13¼ in. [34 cm]

Figures in parentheses refer to larger sizes. One figure refers to all sizes.

YOU WILL NEED

- 8(**9**:10:**11**:12) x 50-g balls of Sirdar Medici in Romeo, shade 162
- J/10 (6.00-mm) crochet hook

GAUGE

12 sts and 13 rows to 4 in. (10 cm) over single crochet using J/10 (6.00-mm) hook. Change hook size if necessary to obtain this gauge.

ABBREVIATIONS

ch = chain stitch; **cont** = continue; **dec** = decrease; **foll** = following; **inc** = increase; **RS** = right side; **sc** = single crochet; **2sctog** = insert hook in first st, yo and pull through, insert hook in 2nd st, yo and pull through, yo and pull through 3 loops on hook; **ss** = slip stitch; **st(s)** = stitch(es); **tr** = triple; **WS** = wrong side; **yo** = yarn over hook; **[ ]** = work instructions in brackets as directed.

NOTES

- The sweater is worked from the top downward so that the chain edge is at the shoulders, and the increases for the ruffle make the lower edge flute.
- The chain at the beginning of sc rows is not worked into or counted as a stitch.
- Mark the last increase row of the back and front armholes and the sleeve top.

TIPS

- Check your gauge carefully. With a textured yarn like this, it's best to work loosely; if you pull the stitches tight, the fabric will close up and affect the size of your sweater.
- Make the starting chain loosely. If you pull the chain stitches tight, it will be hard to see where to place the hook, because of the varying thickness of the yarn.
- Hold your work up to the light of a window to count stitches or rows.
- The stitch pattern looks the same on both sides, so mark the RS with a contrast loop of smooth thread to help you see at a glance which is the right side.
- Place markers as a reminder for counting rows when shaping.

BACK

Make 42(**44**:46:**48**:50)ch.
Row 1 (RS) 1sc in 2nd ch from hook, [1sc in each ch] to end. 41(**43**:45:**47**:49) sts.
Row 2 1ch, [1sc in each sc] to end.
Row 2 forms sc. Cont in sc, work 14 more rows.
Shape armholes. Inc row (RS) 1ch, 2sc in 1st sc, [1sc in each sc] to last sc, 2sc in last sc.
Cont in sc, inc in this way at each end of next 4(**5**:6:**7**:8) RS rows. 51(**55**:59:**63**:67) sts.
** Work 11 rows straight.
Shape sides. Dec row (RS) 1ch, 1sc in 1st sc, 2sctog, [1sc in each sc] to last 3sc, 2sctog, 1sc in last sc.
Cont in sc, dec in this way at each end of 2 foll 6th rows. 45(**49**:53:**57**:61) sts.
Work 22 rows straight, ending with a RS row.
Ruffle row (WS) 1sc in 1st sc, 3ch, [3tr in next sc, 1tr in foll sc] to end.
Fasten off. Darn in ends.

FRONT

Right side Make 8(**9**:10:**11**:12)ch.
Row 1 (RS) 1sc in 2nd ch from hook, [1sc in each ch] to end. 7(**8**:9:**10**:11) sts.
Row 2 1ch, [1sc in each sc] to end.
Row 2 forms sc. Cont in sc, work 10 more rows ***.
Shape neck. Inc row 1 (RS) 1ch, [1sc in each sc] to last sc, 2sc in last sc.
Inc row 2 1ch, 2sc in 1st sc, [1sc in each sc] to end.
Cont in sc, inc in this way at neck edge on next 2 rows.
Next row (RS) 1ch, 2sc in 1st sc, [1sc in each sc] to last sc, 2sc in last sc.
13(**14**:15:**16**:17) sts. Fasten off.
Left side Work as given for right side to ***.
Shape neck. Inc row 1 (RS) 1ch, 2sc in 1st sc, [1sc in each sc] to end.
Inc row 2 1ch, [1sc in each sc] to last sc, 2sc in last sc.
Cont in sc, inc in this way at neck edge on next 2 rows.

This simple top is demure enough for daytime but pretty enough for parties.

Next row (RS) 1ch, 2sc in 1st sc, [1sc in each sc] to last sc, 2sc in last sc.
13(**14**:15:**16**:17) sts.
Joining row (WS) 1ch, [1sc in each sc] of left side, 17ch, [1sc in each sc] of right side.
Next row (RS) 1ch, 2sc in 1st sc, 1sc in each of next 12(**13**:14:**15**:16)sc, 1sc in each of next 17ch, 1sc in each of next 12(**13**:14:**15**:16)sc, 2sc in last sc. 45(**47**:49:**51**:53) sts.
Cont in sc, inc as before at each end of next 3(**4**:5:**6**:7) RS rows. 51(**55**:59:**63**:67) sts.
Complete as given for back from ** to end.
Darn in ends.

SLEEVES

Make 14(**16**:18:**20**:22)ch.
Row 1 (RS) 1sc in 2nd ch from hook, [1sc in each ch] to end. 13(**15**:17:**19**:21) sts.
Shape top. Next row 1ch, 2sc in 1st sc, [1sc in each sc] to last sc, 2sc in last sc.

Cont in sc, inc in this way at each end of next 6(**7**:8:**9**:10) rows, then inc at each end of next 5 RS rows. 37(**41**:45:**49**:53) sts.
Shape sleeve Cont in sc, work 11(**7**:3:**7**:5) rows.
Dec row (RS) 1ch, 1sc in 1st sc, 2sctog, [1sc in each sc] to last 3sc, 2sctog, 1sc in last sc.
Cont in sc, dec in this way at each end of 3(**4**:5:**6**:7) foll 6th(**6th**:6th:**4th**:4th) rows. 29(**31**:33:**35**:37) sts.
Work 12(**10**:8:**10**:8) rows, ending with a RS row.
Work ruffle row as given for back. Fasten off.
Darn in ends.

NECK EDGING

Matching sts, join shoulders. Join yarn at right shoulder seam.
Round 1 (RS) 1ch, 1sc in each of 27ch across back neck, 17sc in row ends down left front neck, 1sc in each of 17ch across front neck and 17sc in row ends up right front neck, ss in first sc, turn. 78 sts.
Round 2 1ch, 1sc in each of first 3 sc, [2sctog, 1sc in each of next 4 sc] 3 times, 2sctog, 1sc in each of next 5 sc, [2sctog, 1sc in each of next 4 sc] 5 times, 2sctog, 1sc in each of next 9 sc, 2sctog, 1sc in each of next 4 sc, 2sctog, 1sc in last sc, ss in first sc, turn. 66 sts.
Round 3 1ch, [1sc in each sc] to end, ss in first sc, turn.
Round 4 1sc in first sc, 3ch, 3tr in next sc, [1tr in next sc, 3tr in foll sc] to end, ss in 3rd ch. Fasten off. Darn in ends.

TO FINISH

Matching underarm markers, sew in sleeve tops. Join side and sleeve seams. Darn in ends.

Textured Cardigan Coat

All you need to make this amazing coat is chain stitch and single crochet. It is worked in one piece to the armholes, then divided and worked straight for back and fronts. The sleeves are almost straight pieces with fold-back cuffs. The yarn shades gently in color, creating a soft, striped effect as you crochet. Wrap over and pin or belt the coat or add pom-poms and leave it open.

ESTIMATED TIME TO COMPLETE
For the coat, 30 hours, including the pom-poms.

ABOUT THIS YARN
Noro Silk Garden is a lightweight yarn with a hand-spun effect. It's a mix of 45 percent silk, 45 percent kid mohair and 10 percent lamb's wool and has approximately 111 yd. (100 m) to a 50-g ball.

SIZES
To fit: bust 34–38(**40–44**) in. [86–97(**102–112**) cm]
Actual measurements: bust 45(**50¾**) in. [114(**131**) cm]; length 33½(**34¼**) in. [85(**87**) cm]; **sleeve** (before folding cuff back) 19 in. [48 cm].
Figures in parentheses refer to larger size. One figure refers to all sizes.

YOU WILL NEED
- 18(**21**) x 50-g balls of Noro Silk Garden in shade 226
- M/13 (9.00-mm) crochet hook

GAUGE
8 [1sc, 1ch, 1sc] groups to 6 in. (15 cm), 10 rows to 4 in. (10 cm) over pattern using M/13 (9.00-mm) hook. Change hook size if necessary to obtain this gauge.

ABBREVIATIONS
ch = chain; **cont** = continue; **inc** = increase; **patt** = pattern; **rep** = repeat; **RS** = right side; **sc** = single crochet; **ss** = slip stitch; **[ ]** = work instructions in brackets as directed.

TIPS

■ The hook size is larger than usual for this weight of yarn so the stitch pattern is very open; be sure to check your gauge carefully.

■ Once you get going, this is definitely a project for cold evenings as the back and fronts will act as a lap blanket! If you want to carry work around, crochet the sleeves.

■ Pom-poms are optional; if you don't want them you'll need one less ball of yarn.

■ If you prefer to make an afghan or wrap, work as given for back and fronts until about 1½ balls of yarn are left. Finish edges with two rounds of sc in same way as the coat. Use any spare yarn for pom-poms.

BACK AND FRONTS

Make 184(**208**)ch loosely.
Row 1 (RS) * Miss 2ch, [1sc, 1ch, 1sc] in next ch, rep from * to last ch, 1sc in last ch. 61(**69**) groups.
Row 2 1ch, skip first sc, * [1sc, 1ch, 1sc] in next sc, skip 1ch and 1sc, rep from * to end, 1sc in last ch.
Row 2 forms the patt. Cont in patt, work 58 more rows.
Right front. Next row (RS) 1ch, skip first sc, * [1sc, 1ch, 1sc] in next sc, skip 1ch and 1sc, rep from * 14(**16**) more times, 1sc in next sc, turn and complete right front on these 15(**17**) groups. Patt 23(**25**) more rows. Fasten off.

Back With RS facing, join yarn to 2nd sc of group at right armhole.

Next row (RS) 1ch, * [1sc 1ch, 1sc] in next sc, skip 1ch and 1sc, rep from * 28(**32**) more times, 1sc in next sc, turn and complete back on these 29(**33**) groups. Patt 23(**25**) more rows. Fasten off.

Left front With RS facing, join yarn in 2nd sc of group at left armhole.

Next row (RS) 1ch, * [1sc, 1ch, 1sc] in next sc, skip 1ch and 1sc, rep from * 14(**16**) more times, 1sc in last ch. Complete left front on these 15(**17**) groups. Patt 23(**25**) more rows. Fasten off. Darn in all ends.

SLEEVES

Make 61(**70**)ch loosely.

Work Row 1 as given for back and fronts. 20(**23**) groups.

Cont in patt as given for back and fronts, work 24 rows.

Inc row 1ch, skip first sc, [1sc, 1ch, 1sc] in each of next 3 sc, patt to end, work [1sc, 1ch, 1sc] in last sc, 1sc in last ch. 22(**25**) groups. Patt 11 rows. Work inc row again. 24(**27**) groups. Patt 10 rows. Fasten off. Darn in all ends.

TO FINISH

Press according to ball band. Join 10(**11**) groups of back to each front for shoulders. Join sleeve seams, reversing seams for 12 rows at lower edge for turn back cuffs. Set in sleeves.

Edgings With RS facing, join yarn at lower edge of left front, work 123(**139**)sc along lower edge of left front, back, and right front, work 2 more sc in same place as last sc for corner, work 84(**86**)sc up right front, 3sc in corner, 10(**12**)sc along right front neck edge, 23(**27**)sc across back neck, 10(**12**)sc along left front edge, 3sc in corner and 84(**86**)sc down left front edge, 2sc in same place as first sc, ss in first sc, turn. Working 3sc in each corner sc, work 1 more round of sc. Fasten off. Working 41(**47**)sc on first round, finish lower edges of sleeves in the same way. Turn cuffs back.

Make 15 x 2 in. (5 cm) pom-poms. Sew 5 along neck edge and 5 on each front.

Pink Flower Top

Although it's made in 4ply cotton, several tricks make this top fast to finish. Each petal of the flower motif is made up of three double triples clustered together and worked straight into the starting ring with chain links between petals, so in just one round you will have completed a motif. The motifs are joined as you work to make an open, lacy fabric, so you will see the top grow quickly.

ESTIMATED TIME TO COMPLETE

Making and joining each flower motif, around 6 minutes, and there are 138 motifs in the top plus the edging; total time taken, 15 hours.

ABOUT THIS YARN

This 4ply cotton is a mercerized machine-washable yarn with a firm twist. It is 100 percent cotton and has approximately 370 yd. (338 m) to a 100-g ball.

SIZES

To fit: bust 32–34(**36–38**) in. [81–86(**91–97**) cm]
Actual measurements: bust 34½(**37¾**) in. [88(**96**) cm];
length 21(22¾) in. [53(**58**) cm]
Figures in parentheses refer to larger size. One figure refers to all sizes.

YOU WILL NEED

- 2 x 100-g balls of 4ply cotton
- C/2(**D/3**) [2.50(**3.00**)-mm] crochet hook

GAUGE

Each flower motif measures 2⅛(2⅜) in. [5.5(**6**) cm] when pressed, using C/2(**D/3**) [2.50(**3.00**)-mm] hook. Change hook size if necessary to obtain this gauge.

ABBREVIATIONS

ch = chain; **cont** = continue; **dtr** = double triple; **3dtrtog** = leaving last loop of each stitch on hook, work 3 double triples, yo and pull through 4 loops on hook; **RS** = right side; **sc** = single crochet; **sp(s)** = space(es); **ss** = slip stitch; **st** = stitch; **WS** = wrong side; **yo** = yarn over hook; [ ] = work instructions in brackets as directed.

NOTES

- The motifs are joined in rounds for the back and front to the armholes; then motifs and joins are omitted to shape the armholes and neck.
- Join the motifs with WS together; RS of the motif you're working on facing you.

TIPS

- If your motif is too big, try again using a smaller hook. If it's too small, try using a larger hook. The correct gauge is important here because the top is sized by using a larger hook to work larger motifs for the 2nd size, so even a small difference in motif size means a large difference to the size of the finished garment. The hook size given is only a guide.
- To work a double triple, take the yarn over the hook three times before inserting the hook and working off the loops one at a time.
- Turn the top inside out and give it a quick burst with spray starch before pressing for a really nice finish.

BACK AND FRONTS

First line of motifs. First flower motif
Wind yarn around finger to form a ring.
Round 1 (RS) 5ch, leaving last loop of each st on hook, work 2dtr in ring, yo and pull through 3 loops on hook, 7ch, [3dtrtog in ring, 7ch] 5 times, ss in 5th ch. Fasten off. Darn in ends.
2nd flower motif Work as First flower motif until 6 petals have been completed, 3ch, 1sc in a 7ch sp of First flower motif, 3ch, ss in 5th ch. Fasten off. Darn in ends. Cont working motifs, joining each one in the 7ch sp opposite the previous join until a line of 15 motifs has been completed.
16th flower motif Work as First flower motif until 3 petals have been completed, join in 15th motif, work 3 more petals, join in first motif to make a round.
2nd line of motifs. First flower motif
Work until 5 petals have been completed, join in 7ch sp to the right of top petal of first motif, work one petal, join in 7ch sp at left of top petal of 2nd motif.
2nd flower motif Work until 4 petals have been completed, join in previous motif, then in 2nd and 3rd motifs of first line of motifs.
Cont joining in this way until 15 motifs have been joined.
16th flower motif Work until 3 petals have been completed, join in 15th motif, last 2 sps of first line and in first motif of 2nd line between each of the last 3 petals.
Cont making and joining motifs in this way until 6 lines of motifs have been completed.
Shape armholes and neck. 7th line of motifs Make and join 7 motifs, skip one motif, [make and join 3 motifs, skip one motif] twice.
Back Cont on 7 motifs, join 8 motifs for 8th line of motifs and 7 motifs for 9th line of motifs.
Left and right fronts Cont on 3 motifs at each side. Placing motifs so neck hole is wider each time, join 3 motifs at each side for 8th line of motifs and 2 motifs at each side for 9th line of motifs. Join fronts to back

with 2 motifs at each side.
Neck edging With RS facing, join yarn in 7ch sp of right back neck motif.
Round 1 (RS) 1ch, [7sc in 7ch sp, 4ch, 7sc in next 7ch sp] 4 times, [4ch, 7sc in each of next two 7ch sps] 4 times, [4ch, 7sc in next 7ch sp] twice, [4ch, 7sc in each of next two 7ch sps] 4 times, 4ch.
Round 2 Ss in first sc, [4ch, ss in 1st ch, ss in each of next 2 sc] 3 times, ss in 4ch sp, 4ch, ss in 1st ch, ss in 4ch sp, cont working

picots with ss between in this way to end of round, ss in first ss. Fasten off.
Armhole edgings With RS facing, join yarn at underarms and complete to match neck edging.
Lower edging With RS facing, join yarn in sp level with underarm and complete to match neck edging.

TO FINISH

Darn in all ends. Press according to ball band.

Cream-Flowered Tunic

This tunic is made from the same easy-to-work-and-join one-round motifs as the Pink Flower Top on page 78, but the longer, looser-fitting simple T-shape gives a very different effect. Wear this over a plain dress for a party or layer it over a sweater for a pretty look on cooler days.

ESTIMATED TIME TO COMPLETE

Each motif, 6 minutes; for the first-size tunic 40 hours, including edging.

ABOUT THIS YARN

Sirdar Pure Cotton 4ply is a smooth, firmly twisted 100 percent cotton yarn with 370 yd. (338 m) to a 100-g ball.

SIZES

TO FIT: bust 32 to 34(**36 to 38**) in. [81 to 86(**91 to 97**) cm]

Actual measurements: bust 39(**42½**) in. [99(**108**) cm]; **length** 31½(**34½**) in. [80(**87.5**) cm]; **sleeve** 17½(**19**) in. [44.5(**48.5**) cm]

Figures in parentheses refer to larger sizes. One figure refers to all sizes.

YOU WILL NEED

■ 4(**5**) x 100-g balls of Sirdar Pure Cotton 4ply in cream, shade 021

■ C/2(**D/3**) [2.50(**3.00**)-mm] crochet hook

GAUGE

Each motif measures 2⅛(**2⅜**) in. [5.5(**6**) cm] using C/2(**D/3**) [2.50(**3.00**)-mm] hook. Change hook size if necessary to obtain this size motif.

ABBREVIATIONS

ch = chain; **cont** = continue; **dtr** = double triple; **3dtrtog** = leaving last loop of each st on hook, work 3 dtr, yo and pull through 4 loops on hook; **rep** = repeat; **RS** = right side; **sc** = single crochet; **sp** = space; **ss** = slip stitch; **st(s)** = stitch(es); **WS** = wrong side; **yo** = yarn over hook; [ ] = work instructions in brackets as directed.

TIPS

■ If you prefer, rather than winding the yarn around your finger you could start each motif with 5ch, then ss in first ch to form a ring. It is a bit easier to work into a chain ring but the centers of the motifs won't be as small.

■ To fasten off the motifs neatly don't use chain stitch; cut the end and pull it through after working the last stitch, then darn the end in to join the round.

BACK AND FRONT

First line of motifs Work as given for Pink Flower Top (see page 78) until 17 motifs have been completed. Join in a ring with 18th motif in same way as given for 16th motif of Pink Flower Top.

Cont making and joining motifs in same way as camisole until 11 rounds of motifs have been completed.

Front and sleeves. First line of motifs (RS) Make and join 8 motifs in a row for left sleeve, make and join 9 motifs across front, make and join 8 motifs in a row for right sleeve.

2nd line of motifs With RS facing, make and join 24 motifs.

3rd line of motifs With RS facing, make and join 25 motifs.

Neck shaping. Next line of motifs With RS facing, make and join 10 motifs, omit center 4 motifs, make and join 10 motifs.

Back and sleeves Work back in the same way as front until 2nd line of motifs has been completed.

3rd line of motifs Make 10 motifs joining to front and back each time, join next motif to back and one sp of last motif at neck edge, join 3 motifs to back only, join next motif to back and one sp of first motif at neck edge, join last 10 motifs to front and back each time.

JOIN SLEEVES

Left sleeve With WS facing and taking both sides of sleeves together each time, join

yarn to 2nd 7ch sp of motifs at cuff edge, *
2sc in sp, 1sc in 3dtrtog, 2sc in next sp, 7ch,
rep from * 6 more times, 2sc in sp, 1sc in
3dtrtog, 2sc in next sp. Fasten off.
Underarm motif 5ch, ss in first ch to
form a ring, 1ch, 1sc in ring, [* 5ch, 1sc in sc
joining motifs, 5ch *, 1sc in ring] 5 times,
rep from * to *, ss in first sc. Fasten off.
Right sleeve Join and work underarm
motif in same way as left sleeve. Darn in end.

SLEEVE EDGINGS

Fill each space between motifs at cuff edge of
sleeves with a half motif made and joined
until 4 petals of motif have been completed,
work 1dtr in ring, fasten off.
With RS facing, join yarn at sleeve seam.
Round 1 1ch, 2sc in first sp after join, *
[1sc in 3dtrtog, 5sc in next sp] twice, 2sc in
each of next 2 sps, rep from * 5 times, 1sc in
3dtrtog, 5sc in next sp, 1sc in 3dtrtog, 2sc in
last sp, ss in first sc. Fasten off. Darn in ends.

NECK EDGING

With RS facing, join yarn to right-hand
3dtrtog of shoulder motif.
Round 1 1ch, * [1sc in 3dtrtog, 5sc in 7ch
sp] once, 1sc in 3dtrtog, 2ch, rep from *
around neck edge working instructions in
brackets twice across 3 motifs at center back
and front, ending ss in first sc.
Round 2 1ch, [1sc in each sc and 2sc in
each 2ch sp] to end, ss in first sc. Fasten off.

LOWER EDGING

With RS facing, join yarn to right-hand
3dtrtog of motif at left side. Complete to
match neck edging, working instructions in
brackets twice for each rep.

TO FINISH

Darn in all ends. Press according to ball band.

Cover up while showing
your femininity in this
lacy tunic.

Babies
& Children

Rosebud Hairband

You can use these versatile flowers to decorate almost anything. The flowers are just simple loops of chain, so they're quick and easy to make. The leaves take a few more stitches, but they're just as simple. Put them together, and the effect is vibrant and playful.

ESTIMATED TIME TO COMPLETE

Each flower took 10 minutes; hairband took 1 hour 20 minutes.

ABOUT THIS YARN

The type of yarn you choose to make these flowers and leaves will affect the size and character of the motifs. The flowers in the picture are in soft embroidery cotton that has 11 yd. (10 m) to a 5-g hank, the equivalent of a fingering-weight cotton yarn.

SIZE

Each flower 1¼ in. (3 cm); **headband** (from end to end) 14½ in. (37 cm)

YOU WILL NEED

■ small amounts of soft embroidery cotton or fingering-weight cotton yarn in 3 shades of pink (A) and 2 shades of green (B)
■ C/2 (2.50-mm) crochet hook
■ plain black hairband
■ black sewing thread and sharp needle

GAUGE

Each flower measures 1¼ in. (3 cm) across using C/2 (2.50-mm) hook. Change hook size if necessary to obtain this size flower.

ABBREVIATIONS

ch = chain; **hdc** = half-double crochet; **RS** = right side; **sc** = single crochet; **sp** = space; **ss** = slip st; **st** = stitch; **[ ]** = work instructions in brackets as directed.

NOTE

Use one shade of green for all the centers and the other shade of green for the leaves. Vary the order in which you use the different shades of pink for the petals.

TIPS

■ If you don't have the right color yarns in your stash, buy hanks of soft embroidery cotton.
■ You can easily use a different size, width, or color headband; simply vary the numbers of flowers you make to decorate it.
■ You could also use the flowers and leaves to decorate a bracelet or to make a corsage.

FLOWER

Using first shade of B, wind yarn around finger to make a ring.

Round 1 (RS) 1ch, 10sc in ring, pull end to close ring, change to a shade of A, ss in first sc. Cont in first shade of A.

Round 2 1ch, 1sc in same sc as ss, 2ch, skip 1sc, [1sc in next sc, 2ch, skip 1sc] 4 times, ss in first sc.

Round 3 [Ss in next sp, 5ch, ss in same sp] 5 times. Fasten off.

Join 2nd shade of A in a 2ch sp of 2nd round, behind a 5ch loop of 3rd round and between the 2 ss.

Round 4 1ch, 1sc in same sp, [5ch, 1sc in between ss in next sp] 4 times, 5ch, ss in first sc. Fasten off. Darn in all ends.

Varying the shades of A, make 4 more flowers.

LEAF

Using 2nd shade of B, make 9ch.

Row 1 Ss in 2nd ch from hook, 1sc in each

This pretty flowered band is perfect for parties, beautiful for bridesmaids, or ideal for just dressing up.

of next 6ch, 3sc in end ch, 1sc in base of next 6ch, turn.

Row 2 Skip first sc, ss in next sc, 1sc in foll sc, 1hdc in each of next 5sc, 3hdc in foll sc, 1hdc in each of next 5sc, ss in foll sc, turn.

Row 3 Ss in first st, [3ch, ss in next st] 12 times. Fasten off. Darn in all ends. Make another leaf.

TO FINISH

Sew the flowers on top of the hairband. Pinch the leaves to make them curl slightly, and sew one leaf at each side.

Mix and match the colors from your yarn stash to make your own version of this pretty cardigan.

Chevron Cardigan

This jazzy little cardigan has a sweet flared shape and bell sleeves. The wavy chevron pattern is in double crochet, making it grow quickly. The fronts and back are worked in one up to the armholes, so you don't need to worry about matching the stripes, and every row of the shaping that flares the body and sleeves is given; mark them as you work to keep your place.

ESTIMATED TIME TO COMPLETE
10 hours

ABOUT THIS YARN
The cardigan is made from a variety of smooth wool-mix sport-weight yarns with around 131 yd. (120 m) to a 50-g ball.

SIZES
To fit: age 1 to 2 years; **chest** 20 to 22 in. (50 to 55 cm)
Actual measurements: chest 22¾ in. (58 cm); **length** 14¼ in. (36 cm); **sleeve** 10 in. (25.5 cm)

YOU WILL NEED
- 150 g of wool-mix DK in lime green (A)
- 75 g of wool-mix DK in shades of pink (B)
- 75 g of wool-mix DK in shades of orange (C)
- E/4 (3.50-mm) crochet hook
- 5 buttons

GAUGE
18 sts and 8½ rows to 4 in. (10 cm) over chevron patt using E/4 (3.50-mm) hook. Change hook size if necessary to obtain this gauge.

ABBREVIATIONS
alt = alternate; **beg** = beginning; **ch** = chain; **cont** = continue; **dc** = double; **hdc** = half-double crochet; **patt** = pattern; **rep** = repeat; **RS** = right side; **sc** = single crochet; **st(s)** = stitch(es); **tr** = triple; **[ ]** = work instructions in brackets as directed.

NOTES
- Yarn amounts are approximate because the sport-weight yarns you use may be a different fiber mix and have a different length to the weight of the yarn.
- Make the starting chain very loosely. If necessary use a larger hook.
- To work in the same way as the colors shown in the picture, use one shade of lime green but vary the shades of pink and orange.
- You can change color for every row or ignore the stripes and work the cardigan all in one color, in which case you'll need approximately 250 g of wool-mix yarn.

TIPS
- For the neatest finish at the front edges, break off the yarn at the end of each color stripe and darn in the ends after working the edging.
- Choose yarns that can be washed and pressed in the same way. Always follow the care code for the most delicate of the yarns you've used.
- If you work in an alternating stripe pattern, it's easy to tell the difference between the right and wrong sides, even though the pattern looks the same, because all rows in A are right-side rows.
- Mark every row of shaping on body and sleeves to keep your place easily.

BACK AND FRONTS

Using A, make 142ch loosely.
Row 1 1sc in 2nd ch from hook, [1sc in each ch] to end. 141 sts.
Row 2 (RS) 1sc in first sc, 2ch, [2dc in next sc, 1dc in each of next 2sc, skip 1sc, 1dc in next sc, skip 1sc, 1dc in each of next 2sc, 2dc in foll sc, 1dc in next sc] 14 times.
Change to B.
Row 3 1sc in first dc, 2ch, [2dc in next dc, 1dc in each of next 2dc, skip 1dc, 1dc in next dc, skip 1dc, 1dc in each of next 2dc, 2dc in foll dc, 1dc in next dc] 14 times.
Row 3 forms the chevron patt.
Cont in chevron patt, working alt stripes of 1 row A, 1 row C, 1 row A, 1 row B, for 8 more rows, ending with a row in B.
Shape sides. Row 1 (RS) Using A, patt 30, ending with 2dc in same dc, * 1dc in

each of next 4dc, skip 1dc, 1dc in next dc, skip 1dc, 1dc in each of next 4dc *, beg 2dc in same dc, patt 59, ending 2dc in same dc, rep from * to *, patt 30. 137 sts.

Row 2 Using C, patt 30, * 1dc in each of next 3dc, skip 1dc, 1dc in next dc, skip 1dc, 1dc in each of next 3dc *, patt 59, rep from * to *, patt 30. 133 sts.

Row 3 Using A, patt 30, * 1dc in each of next 2dc, skip 1dc, 1dc in next dc, skip 1dc, 1dc in each of next 2dc *, patt 59, rep from * to *, patt 30. 129 sts.

Row 4 Using B, patt 30, * [1dc in next dc, skip 1dc] twice, 1dc in next dc *, patt 59, rep from * to *, patt 30. 125 sts.

Row 5 Using A, patt 30, * skip 1dc, 1dc in next dc, skip 1dc *, patt 59, rep from * to *, patt 30. 121 sts.

Row 6 Using C, patt 26, * skip 1dc, 1dc in next dc, 2dc in foll dc, skip 1dc, 1dc in next dc, skip 1dc, 2dc in next dc, 1dc in foll dc, skip 1dc *, patt 51, rep from * to *, patt 26. 117 sts.

Row 7 Using A, patt 26, * skip 1dc, 2dc in next dc, skip 1dc, 1dc in next dc, skip 1dc, 2dc in next dc, skip 1dc *, patt 51, rep from * to *, patt 26. 113 sts.

Row 8 Using B, patt 26, * skip 1dc, 1dc in each of next 3dc, skip 1dc *, patt 51, rep from * to *, patt 26. 109 sts.

Row 9 Using A, patt 26, * skip 1dc, 1dc in next dc, skip 1dc *, patt 51, rep from * to *, patt 26. 105 sts.

Row 10 Using C, patt 26, skip 1dc, patt 51, skip 1dc, patt 26. 103 sts.

Right front. Next row (RS) Using A, patt 26, turn and complete right front on these sts. Cont in chevron stripe patt, work 5 rows. Fasten off.

Shape neck. Next row (RS) Join A in 11th st from front edge, 1sc in same place as join, 2ch, patt to end. 16 sts. Cont in stripe patt, work 4 more rows. Fasten off.

Back With RS facing, join A in next free st.

Row 1 1sc in same place as join, 2ch, patt 50 more sts, turn and complete back on these 51 sts. Patt 9 rows, ending with 1 row less than front to shoulder. Fasten off.

Left front. Row 1 With RS facing, join A in next free st, 1sc in same place as join, 2ch, patt to end. 26 sts. Cont in chevron stripe patt, work 5 rows.

Shape neck. Next row Patt 16, turn. Cont on these 16 sts, work 4 more rows. Fasten off. Darn in all ends.

SLEEVES

Using A, make 42ch loosely.

Work Row 1 as given for back and fronts. 41 sts.

Cont in chevron stripe patt as given for back and fronts, work 8 rows.

First dec row (RS) Using A, 1sc in first dc, 2ch, 1dc in each of next 3dc, skip 1dc, 1dc in next dc, patt to last 5 sts, skip 1dc, 1dc in each of next 3dc, 1dc in 2nd ch. 39 sts.

Next row Using B, 1sc in first dc, 2ch, 2dc in next dc, 1dc in foll dc, skip 1dc, patt to last 4 sts, skip 1dc, 1dc in next dc, 2dc in foll dc, 1dc in 2nd ch.

2nd dec row Using A, 1sc in first dc, 2ch, 1dc in each of next 2dc, skip 1dc, 1dc in next dc, patt to last 4 sts, skip 1dc, 1dc in each of next 2dc, 1dc in 2nd ch. 37 sts.

Next row Using C, 1sc in first dc, 2ch, 2dc in next dc, skip 1dc, 1dc in next dc, patt to last 3 sts, skip 1dc, 2dc in next dc, 1dc in 2nd ch.

3rd dec row Using A, 1sc in first dc, 2ch, 1dc in next dc, skip 1dc, 1dc in next dc, patt to last 3 sts, skip 1dc, 1dc in next dc, 1dc in 2nd ch. 35 sts.

Next row Using B, 1sc in first dc, 2ch, 1dc in same place as sc, skip 1dc, 1dc in next dc, patt to last 2 sts, skip 1dc, 2dc in 2nd ch.

4th dec row Using A, 1sc in first dc, 2ch, skip 1dc, 1dc in next dc, patt to last 2 sts, skip 1dc, 1dc in 2nd ch.

Next row Using C, 1sc in first dc, 2ch, 1dc in next dc, patt to last st, 1dc in 2nd ch. 33 sts.

First inc row Using A, 1sc in first dc, 2ch, 1dc in same place as sc, 1dc in next dc, patt to last st, 2dc in 2nd ch. 35 sts.

2nd inc row Using B, 1sc in first dc, 2ch, 2dc in next dc, 1dc in next dc, patt to last 2

sts, 2dc in next dc, 1dc in 2nd ch. 37 sts.

3rd inc row Using A, 1sc in first dc, 2ch, 2dc in next dc, 1dc in each of foll 2 dc, patt to last 3 sts, 1dc in next dc, 2dc in foll dc, 1dc in 2nd ch. 39 sts.

4th inc row Using C, 1sc in first dc, 2ch, 2dc in next dc, 1dc in each of foll 3 dc, patt to last 4 sts, 1dc in each of next 2dc, 2dc in foll dc, 1dc in 2nd ch. 41 sts.

Change to A.

First finishing row 1sc in first dc, 2ch, [2dc in next dc, 1dc in each of foll 2dc, skip 1dc, 1tr in next dc, skip 1dc, 1dc in each of next 2dc, 2dc in foll dc, 1dc in next st] to end.

2nd finishing row 1ch, [1sc in each st] to end. Fasten off.

EDGING

Matching sts, join shoulders.

Row 1 (RS) Join A at lower edge of right front, work 52sc in row ends up right front edge, 2sc in corner, 1sc in each of 6dc along right front neck, 1hdc in next dc, 1dc in each of foll 2dc, 1hdc and 1sc in first row end up right front neck, 2sc in each of next 3 row ends, 1hdc and 1dc in last row end, 1sc in each of first 2 free dc of back neck, * 1hdc in next dc, skip 1dc, 1dc in next dc, skip 1dc,

1hdc in foll dc *, 1sc in each of next 5dc, rep from * to *, 1sc in each of next 2 dc, 1dc and 1hdc in first row end of left front neck, 2sc in each of next 3 row ends, 1sc and 1hdc in last row end, 1dc in each of first 2dc along left front neck, 1hdc in next dc, 1sc in each of next 6dc, 2sc in corner, 52sc in row ends down left front edge. 161 sts.

Row 2 1ch, 1sc in each sc up left front to corner, 2sc in each of 2sc at corner, 1sc in each st around neck, 2sc in each of 2sc at corner, 1sc in each sc down right front. 165 sts.

Buttonhole row 1ch, 1sc in each of first 19sc, 2ch, skip 2sc, [1sc in each of next 6sc, 2ch, skip 2sc] 4 times, 2sc in each of next 2sc, 1sc in each sc around neck, 2sc in each of 2sc at corner, [1sc in each sc] to end.

Row 4 1ch, [1sc in each sc] to corner, 2sc in each of 2sc at corner, [1sc in each sc] around neck, 2sc in each of 2sc at corner, [1sc in each sc and 2sc in each 2ch sp] to end.

Row 5 1ch, [1sc in each sc] to end. Fasten off. Darn in all ends.

TO FINISH

Press according to ball bands. Join sleeve seams and set in sleeves. Sew on buttons.

Pretty Pull-on Hat

This pretty hat couldn't be easier to make. It's all in double crochet, so it grows quickly, and it's worked in rounds from the top down, so there's no sewing required except for the decorative flowers. These are made from strips of double crochet gathered and sewn on afterward.

ESTIMATED TIME TO COMPLETE
For the 2nd-size hat, 4 hours.

ABOUT THIS YARN
Debbie Bliss Cashmerino DK is a soft, smooth mix of 55 percent merino wool, 33 percent microfiber, and 12 percent cashmere. It has approximately 121 yd. (110 m) to a 50-g ball.

SIZES
To fit: age 6 months(**1 to 3**:4 to 5) years)
Actual measurement: around head 14¾(**17¾**:20½) in. [37.5(**45**:52.5) cm]
Figures in parentheses refer to larger sizes. One figure refers to all sizes.

YOU WILL NEED
■ 1(**2**:2) x 50-g balls of Debbie Bliss Cashmerino DK, in pink, shade 005
■ E/4 (3.50-mm) crochet hook

GAUGE
16 sts and 10 rows to 4 in. (10 cm) over double crochet worked in rounds using E/4 (3.50-mm) hook. Change hook size if necessary to obtain this gauge.

ABBREVIATIONS
ch = chain; **cont** = continue; **dc** = double crochet; **ss** = slip stitch; **st(s)** = stitch(es); [ ] = work instructions in brackets as directed.

TIPS
■ The hat is worked from the top down, which makes it easy to check the fit as you go.
■ Work the 3rd chain at the start of each round loosely. This will make it easier to slip the hook under both loops when joining at the end of the round.
■ Crab stitch is just single crochet worked backward. When edging the ruffles for the flowers, work the crab stitch quite loosely so the edge spreads, making the flowers more ruffled.
■ If you want to make the hat without the flowers, you'll need just 1(**1**:2) 50-g balls of Cashmerino DK.

ROSES
(Make 2) **First ruffle** Make 40ch.
Row 1 1dc in 4th ch from hook, [1dc in each ch] to end. 38 sts.
Work 1 row crab st. Fasten off.
2nd ruffle Make 23ch.
Row 1 As Row 1 of first ruffle. 21 sts.
Row 2 3ch, 2dc in first dc, [3dc in each dc] to end, 3dc in top ch. 63 sts.
Work 1 row crab st. Fasten off. Darn in ends.

TO FINISH
Gather smooth edge of first ruffle, roll and secure to make flower center. Gather 2nd ruffle, curl around flower center, and secure. Darn in all ends. Sew roses on hat level with ears.

HAT

Wind yarn around finger to make a ring.
Round 1 (RS) 3ch, 11dc in ring, pull end to tighten ring, ss in 3rd ch. 12 sts.
Round 2 3ch, 1dc in same place as ss, [2dc in next dc] 11 times, ss in 3rd ch. 24 sts.
Round 3 3ch, 1dc in same place as ss, 1dc in next dc, [2dc in foll dc, 1dc in next dc] 11 times, ss in 3rd ch. 36 sts.
Round 4 3ch, 1dc in same place as ss, 1dc in each of next 2 dc, [2dc in foll dc, 1dc in each of next 2dc] 11 times, ss in 3rd ch. 48 sts.
Cont in this way working one more dc between increases each time, work 1(**2**:3) more increase rounds. 60(**72**:84) sts.
Work 8(**10**:12) rounds straight.
Edging Work 1 round crab stitch. Fasten off.

This simple hat is

trimmed with

easy-to-make rosettes.

Create a family heirloom with an exquisite silk coat that's perfect for baby's first special occasion.

Christening Coat

The simplest of stitches in sumptuous silk yarn combined with pretty ribbon give an antique heirloom effect to this traditional long christening coat. The yoke is in firm single crochet, with the sleeves and skirt in double crochet trimmed with eyelet bands and finished with a tiny shell on the cuff and a deep lacy flounce at the hem. You can button the coat either at the back or at the front.

ESTIMATED TIME TO COMPLETE

For the first-size coat, 10 hours.

ABOUT THIS YARN

Debbie Bliss Pure Silk is a single-ply, soft 100 percent silk yarn with approximately 136 yd. (125 m) to a 50-g ball.

SIZES

To fit: age newborn to 3(**3 to 6**) months;
chest 15¾ to 17(**17 to 18**) in. [40 to 43(**43 to 46**) cm]
Actual measurements: chest 18½(**20**) in. [47(**51**) cm];
length 24¾(**25¼**) in. [63(**64.5**) cm]; **sleeve** 6(**7**) in. 15(**18**) cm].
Figures in parentheses refer to larger sizes. One figure refers to all sizes.

YOU WILL NEED

- 7(**8**) x 50-g balls of Debbie Bliss Pure Silk in ecru, shade 03
- E/4 (3.50-mm) and F/5 (4.00-mm) crochet hooks
- 14 small buttons
- 3¼(**3¾**)-yd. 3(**3.5**)-m] length of narrow ribbon

GAUGE

21 sts and 24 rows to 4 in. (10 cm) over single crochet using E/4 (3.50-mm) hook. Change hook size if necessary to obtain this gauge.

ABBREVIATIONS

ch = chain; **cont** = continue; **dc** = double crochet; **3dctog** = leaving last loop of each st on hook, work 3dc, yo and pull though 4 loops on hook; **dec** = decrease; **rep** = repeat; **RS** = right side; **sc** = single crochet; **2sctog** = insert hook in first st, yo and pull through, insert hook in 2nd st, yo and pull through, yo and pull through 3 loops on hook; **sp** = space; **ss** = slip stitch; **st(s)** = stitch(es); **WS** = wrong side; **yo** = yarn over hook; **[ ]** = work instructions in brackets as directed.

TIPS

■ The pure silk yarn varies slightly in thickness giving it a hand-spun look. If you find a slub in a place where it will mask the pattern, cut and rejoin the yarn, then darn in the ends.
■ The coat can be worn on its own or over a long dress or a nightdress. Alternatively, you could line the skirt with fabric.

YOKE

Front Using F/5 (4.00-mm) hook, make 33(**37**)ch.

Change to E/4 (3.50-mm) hook.

Row 1 (WS) 1sc in 2nd ch from hook, [1sc in each ch] to end. 32(**36**) sts.

Row 2 1ch, [1sc in each sc] to end.

Row 2 forms sc. Work 9(**11**) more rows sc.

Left side of neck. Row 1 (RS) 1ch, 1sc in each of first 12(**14**)sc, turn.

1st dec row 2sctog, [1sc in each sc] to end.

2nd dec row 1ch, [1sc in each sc to last 2sc, 2sctog. 10(**12**) sts.

Work first and 2nd dec rows 1(2) more times. 8 sts.

Work 3 rows sc. Fasten off.

Right side of neck With RS facing you, leave center 8sc, join yarn in next sc.

Row 1 1ch, 1sc in same place as join, [1sc in each sc] to end. 12(**14**) sts.

Dec in same way as Rows 1 and 2 of left side of neck on next 4(**6**) rows. 8 sts. Work 3 rows sc. Fasten off.

Left back yoke Using F/5 (4.00-mm) hook, make 17(**19**)ch.

Change to E/4 (3.50-mm) hook. Work Row 1 as given for front. 16(**18**) sts.

Cont in sc, work 18(**22**) more rows. Fasten off.

Right back yoke Work as given for left back. Matching sts, join shoulders with sc. With RS facing, join yarn at right back underarm, make 16ch, fasten off, join end to first st at right front yoke. Join left underarm in the same way.

SKIRT

Using E/4 (3.50-mm) hook, join yarn at right back edge.

First eyelet band. Row 1 (RS) 1ch, ss in base of each of 16(**18**) ch across right back, 16ch at right underarm, 32(**36**)ch across front, 16ch at left underarm and 16(**18**)ch across left back. 96(**104**) sts.

Row 2 4ch, [skip 1ss, 1dc in same ch as next ss, 1ch] to end, omitting last ch.

Row 3 1ch, 1sc in first dc, [1sc in next sp, 1sc in next dc] to end. 97(**105**) sts.

Change to F/5 (4.00-mm) hook.

Row 1 (WS) 1sc in first sc, 2ch, 1dc in same place as sc, [skip 1sc, 3dc in next sc] to last 2sc, skip 1sc, 2dc in last sc. 145(**157**) sts.

Row 2 1sc in first dc, 2ch, [1dc in each dc] to last st, 1dc in 2nd ch.

Row 2 forms dc. Cont in dc, work 13 more rows.

2nd eyelet band. Row 1 (RS) 1ch, [1sc in each dc] to end.

Row 2 1sc in first sc, 3ch, [skip 1sc, 1dc in next sc, 1ch] to end, omitting last ch.

Row 3 1ch, 1sc in first dc, [1sc in next sp, 1sc in next st] to end.

Openwork pattern. Row 1 (WS) 1sc in first sc, 2ch, 2dc in next sc, [skip 1sc, 2dc in

foll sc] to last sc, 1dc in last sc. 146(**158**) sts.

Row 2 1sc in first dc, 2ch, 2dc between first and 2nd dc, [skip 2dc, 2dc between sts] to end, 1dc in 2nd ch. 148(**160**) sts.

Row 3 1sc in first dc, 2ch, [skip 2dc, 2dc between sts] to last 3 sts, skip 2dc, 1dc in 2nd ch. 146(**158**) sts.

Rows 2 and 3 form the openwork patt. Patt 8 more rows.

Edging. 1st size. Row 1 (RS) 1ch, [1sc in each dc] to last st, do not work into 2nd ch.

2nd size. Row 1 (RS) 1ch, 2sc in first dc, 1sc in each dc to last 2 sts, 2sc in each of last 2 st.

Both sizes 145(**161**) sts.

Row 2 1ch, [1sc in each sc] to end.

Row 3 1ch, 1sc in each of first 3sc, [5ch, skip 3sc, 1sc in each of next 5sc] 17(**19**) times, 5ch, skip 3sc, 1sc in each of last 3sc.

Row 4 1ch, 1sc in first sc, 3ch, * skip 2sc, [1sc in 5ch sp, 3ch] 4 times, skip 2sc, 1sc in next sc, rep from * to end.

Row 5 1ch, 1sc in first sc, 3ch, * skip next 3ch sp, [3dctog in next 3ch sp, 3ch] 3 times, 1sc in center sc, rep from * to end, working final sc in last sc.

Row 6 1ch, 1sc in first sc, 2ch, * [3dctog in next 3ch sp, 3ch] 3 times, 3dctog in foll 3ch sp, rep from * to end, 1dc in last sc.

Row 7 1ch, 1sc in first dc, 3ch, * [3dctog in next 3ch sp, 3ch] 3 times, 1sc between next two 3dctog, rep from * ending last rep 1sc in 2nd ch.

Work Rows 6 and 7 two more times.

Last row (WS) [1sc, 4ch, 2sc, 4ch, 1sc] in each 3ch sp to end. Fasten off.

SLEEVES

Using E/4 (3.50-mm) hook, and with RS facing, work 40(**48**)sc in row ends along armhole edge.

Row 1 (WS) 4ch, [skip 1sc, 1dc in next sc, 1ch] to end, omitting last ch.

Row 2 1ch, [1sc in next dc, 1sc in next sp] to end, 1sc in 3rd ch. 41(**49**) sts.

Change to F/5 (4.00-mm) hook.

Row 3 1sc in first sc, 2ch, [1dc in each sc]

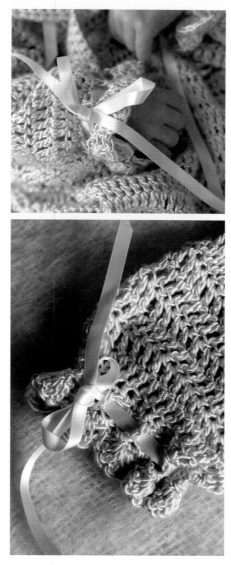

to end. Cont in dc patt, work 12(**14**) rows.

Eyelet band. Row 1 (RS) 1ch, [1sc in each dc] to last st, 1sc in 2nd ch.

Row 2 1sc in first sc, 3ch, skip first dc, [skip 1sc, 1dc in next sc, 1ch] to end.

Row 3 1sc in first dc, [1sc in next sp, 1sc in next dc] to end, working last sc in 2nd ch.

Row 4 1ch, 1sc in first sc, [skip 1sc, 4dc in next sc, skip 1sc, 1sc in next sc] to end. Fasten off. Darn in ends.

NECK EDGING

Using E/4 (3.50-mm) hook and with RS facing, join yarn at left back neck edge, work 8(**10**)sc across left back neck, 9(**11**)sc in row ends down left front neck, 8sc across front neck, 9(**11**)sc in row ends up right front neck and 8(**10**)sc across right back neck. 42(**50**) sts.

Next row (WS) 1ch, 2sc in first sc, 1sc in each sc to last sc, 2sc in last sc. 44(**52**) sts.

Change to F/5 (4.00-mm) hook.

Row 1 1sc in first sc, 2ch, 1dc in same place as first sc, 1dc in each of next 2sc, [3dc in next sc, 1dc in each of foll 3sc] 10(**12**) times, 1dc in last sc. 65(**77**) sts.

Rows 2 and 3 1sc in first dc, 2ch, [1dc in each dc] to end.

Row 4 1ch, [1sc in each dc] to last st, 1sc in 2nd ch.

Row 5 1ch, 1sc in first sc, [skip 1sc, 4dc in next sc, skip 1sc, 1sc in next sc] to end. Fasten off by enlarging loop and passing ball of yarn through, work 8sc in row ends of collar, turn and work 1 row sc, then work two shells in same way as Row 5. Finish the other edge in the same way. Darn in ends.

BUTTONHOLE BAND

Using E/4 (3.50-mm) hook, join yarn at lower edge of left back. Work 96(**100**)sc evenly in row ends up left back.

Buttonhole row (WS) 1ch, 1sc in first sc, [1ch, skip 1sc, 1sc in each of next 6sc] 13 times, 1ch, skip 1sc, 1sc in each of last 3(**7**)sc.

Next row 1ch, [1sc in each sc and in each sp] to end. Work 1 more row sc. Fasten off. Darn in ends.

BUTTON BAND

Work as buttonhole band but join yarn at right back neck and omit buttonholes.

TO FINISH

Press according to ball band. Join row ends at top of sleeves to chain at underarms, then join sleeve seams. Thread ribbon through eyelets around yoke, stitch at underarms and tie in a bow at front. Thread ribbon through cuffs and tie. Thread ribbon through eyelet bands in skirt and at top of sleeves and stitch at each end. Join ends of bands to collar. Sew on buttons.

Heirloom Bonnet

This old-fashioned bonnet involves the same simple stitches as the Christening Coat on page 92. The shape is very simple, too, so it's easy and quick to make.

ESTIMATED TIME TO COMPLETE

2½ hours

ABOUT THIS YARN

See Christening Coat on page 92.

SIZE

To fit: age newborn to 6 months
Actual measurement: around brim
13½ in. (34 cm)

YOU WILL NEED

■ 1 x 50-g ball of Debbie Bliss Pure Silk in ecru, shade 03
■ E/4 (3.50-mm) and F/5 (4.00-mm) crochet hooks
■ 24-in. (60-cm) length of narrow ribbon

GAUGE

15 sts and 13 rows to 4 in. (10 cm) over double-groups patt using F/5 (4.00-mm) hook. Change hook size if necessary to obtain this gauge.

ABBREVIATIONS

See Christening Coat on page 92.

TIPS

■ If you want longer ties, make more chain at each side of the lower edging.
■ You can fold back the shell edging if desired, to make a pretty brim to frame the baby's face.

BONNET

Using F/5 (4.00-mm) hook, make 5ch, ss in first ch to form a ring. Pull yarn to tighten ring.

Row 1 1ch, 7sc in ring, turn.

Row 2 (RS) 1sc in first sc, 2ch, 2dc in same place as sc, [3dc in each sc] to end. 21 sts.

Row 3 1ch, 1sc in first dc, [2ch, skip 1dc, 1sc in next dc] 9 times, 2ch, skip 1dc, 1sc in 2nd ch.

Row 4 1sc in first sc, 2ch, 3dc in each 2ch sp, 1dc in last sc. 32 sts.

Row 5 3ch, [skip 1dc, 1sc in next dc, 2ch] 15 times, 1sc in 2nd ch.

Row 6 As Row 4, working last dc in first ch.

Row 7 As Row 5, repeating instructions in brackets 24 times.

Row 8 As Row 6. 77 sts.

Row 9 1sc in first dc, 2ch, skip first 4dc, [2dc between each 3dc group] to last 4 sts, skip 3dc, 1dc in 2nd ch. 50 sts.

Row 10 1sc in first dc, 2ch, 2dc between first dc and first 2dc group, [2dc between each 2dc group] to end, 2dc after last 2dc group, 1dc in 2nd ch. 52 sts.

Row 11 1sc in first dc, 2ch, skip first 3dc, [2dc between each 2dc group] to end, skip 2dc, 1dc in 2nd ch. 50 sts.

Work Rows 10 and 11 rows 3 more times.

Row 18 1ch, [1sc in each dc] to end, 1sc in ch.

Row 19 4ch, [skip 1sc, 1dc in next sc, 1ch] to end, omitting last ch.

Row 20 1ch, 1sc in first dc, [1sc in next sp, 1sc in next dc] to end, working last sc in 3rd ch. 51 sts.

Row 21 1ch, 1sc in each of first 2sc, [skip 1sc, 4dc in next sc, skip 1sc, 1sc in foll sc] 12 times, 1sc in last sc. Fasten off. Darn in ends.

TIES

Join first 8 rows to form back seam. Using F/5 (4.00-mm) hook, make 40ch, change to E/4 (3.50-mm) hook and with RS facing, work 44sc along lower edge of bonnet, change to F/5 (4.00-mm) hook, make 41ch. Change to E/4 (3.50-mm) hook.

Row 1 1sc in 2nd ch from hook, 1sc in each of next 39ch, 1sc in each of 44sc, 1sc in each of last 40ch. 124 sts.

Work 3 rows sc. Fasten off. Darn in ends.

TO FINISH

Press according to ball band. Making tiny bows at each side, thread ribbon through eyelet band, stitching at each end to secure the bows.

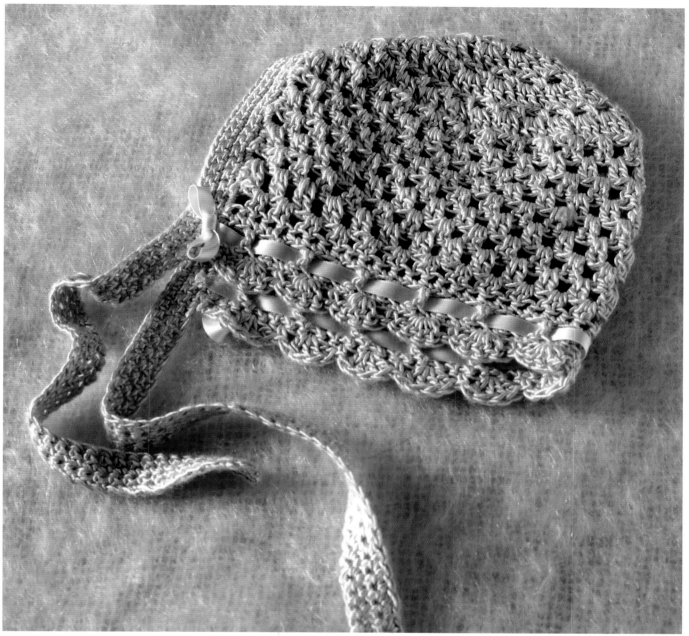

Silk yarn is ideal to make a wonderfully soft bonnet to match the coat.

Heirloom Bootees

These charming little bootees are worked in the round from the toes upward, in single crochet with a shell edging to match the Christening Coat and Heirloom Bonnet on pages 92–97.

ESTIMATED TIME TO COMPLETE

4 hours for the pair

ABOUT THIS YARN

See Christening Coat on page 92.

SIZE

To fit: newborn to 6 months

Actual measurements: along sole

3½ in. (9 cm)

YOU WILL NEED

■ 1 x 50-g ball of Debbie Bliss Pure Silk in ecru, shade 03
■ E/4 (3.50-mm) crochet hook
■ 24 in. (61-cm) length of narrow ribbon

GAUGE

21 sts and 24 rows to 4 in. (10 cm) over single crochet using E/4 (3.50-mm) hook. Change hook size if necessary to obtain this gauge.

ABBREVIATIONS

See Christening Coat on page 92.

TIP

If you'd like to make the bootees longer or shorter in the foot and at the ankle, simply work an even number of rows until you reach the length you require.

BOOTEES

Left bootee Make 8ch.

Round 1 2sc in 2nd ch from hook, 1sc in each of next 5ch, 4sc in last ch, cont working into base of ch, 1sc in each of next 5ch, 2sc in last ch, ss in first sc. 18 sts.

Round 2 1ch, 2sc in first sc, 1sc in each of next 7sc, 2sc in each of foll 2sc, 1sc in each of next 7sc, 2sc in last sc, ss in first sc. 22 sts.

Round 3 1ch, 2sc in first sc, 1sc in each of next 9sc, 2sc in each of foll 2sc, 1sc in each of next 9sc, 2sc in last sc, ss in first sc. 26 sts.

Round 4 1ch, 1sc in same place as ss, [1sc in each sc] to end, ss in first sc, turn. Cont in sc and turning each time, work 15 more rounds **.

Heel opening. Round 1 (RS) Make 14ch loosely, skip 13sc, 1sc in each of next 13sc, ss in first ch, turn.

Round 2 1ch, 1sc in each of 13sc, 1sc in each of next 13ch, ss in first sc, turn. 26 sts. Cont in sc turning each time, work 3 rounds.

Eyelet round (WS) 1sc in first sc, 3ch, skip 1sc, [1dc in next sc, 1ch, skip 1sc] to end, ss in 2nd ch, turn.

Next round 1ch, 1sc in same place as ss, [1sc in next sp, 1sc in next dc] to last sp, 1sc in last sp, ss in first sc, turn. Work 1sc, turn.

Inc round (RS) 1ch, 1sc in each of first 2sc, * [2sc in next sc, 1sc in each of next 3sc] twice, 2sc in foll sc *, 1sc in each of next 4sc,

rep from * to *, 1sc in each of last 2sc, ss in first sc, turn. 32 sts.

Edging round 1ch, [skip 1sc, 4dc in next sc, skip 1sc, 1sc in next sc] to end, ss in first ch. Fasten off.

Heel With RS facing, join yarn in base of first ch at heel opening.

Round 1 (RS) 1ch, 1sc in same place as join, 1sc in base of each of next 12ch, 1sc in each of next 13sc, ss in first sc, turn. 26 sts. Work 1sc, turn.

Round 3 1ch, 2sctog, 1sc in each of next 9sc, [2sctog] twice, 1sc in each of next 9sc, 2sctog, ss in first st, turn. 22 sts.

Round 4 1ch, 2sctog, 1sc in each of next 7sc, [2sctog] twice, 1sc in each of next 7sc, 2sctog, ss in first st. 18 sts. Fasten off.

Right bootee Work as left bootee to **.

Heel opening. Round 1 1ch, 1sc in each of 13sc, make 13ch loosely, ss in first sc, turn.

Round 2 1ch, 1sc in each of next 13ch, 1sc in each of next 13sc, ss in first sc, turn. 26 sts.

Complete as given for left bootee.

TO FINISH

Join 9 sts from each side to close heel seams. Darn in ends. Cut ribbon in half, thread through eyelet rounds, and tie at front.

These lovely little bootees make a
perfect welcome-to-the-world present.

Lacy Victorian Shawl

Although this shawl looks complex, all of the stitches are quite simple; the old-fashioned froth-of-lace effect is achieved by piling on the patterning. There are four center panels worked in a two-row cluster-fan pattern, then joined with a lacy chain zigzag before adding an openwork edging. Make in a soft white for an heirloom baby shawl that will be handed down through the generations.

ESTIMATED TIME TO COMPLETE

For one center strip, 3½ hours; shawl 24 hours.

ABOUT THIS YARN

The yarn used for the shawl is a classic, soft, pure wool fingering with around 200 yd. (183 m) to a 50-g ball.

SIZE

Width 41¾ in. (106 cm); **length** 41¾ in. (106 cm)

YOU WILL NEED

■ 8 x 50-g balls of pure wool fingering-weight yarn in warm white
■ F/5 (4.00-mm) crochet hook

GAUGE

Two patterns across and 8 rows to 4 in. (10 cm) using F/5 (4.00-mm) hook. Change hook size if necessary to obtain this gauge.

ABBREVIATIONS

ch = chain; **dc** = double crochet; **patt(s)** = pattern(s); **rep** = repeat; **RS** = right side; **sc** = single crochet; **sp(s)** = space(s); **ss** = slip stitch; **st(s)** = stitch(es); **tr** = triple; **3trcl** = leaving last loop on the hook each time, work 3tr, yo and pull through 4 loops on hook; **triple 3trcl** = [3trcl, 3ch, 3trcl, 3ch, 3trcl] all in same sp; **WS** = wrong side; [ ] = work instructions in brackets as directed.

TIPS

■ Pure wool is the traditional choice for this kind of lacy shawl. You can use any brand of yarn, but do check the number of yards (meters) to a 50-g ball and adjust the amount of yarn you need if necessary.
■ If you don't have a large blocking board, block the shawl on a carpet or strip the bed and use the mattress covered with a sheet; do this in the morning so the shawl will be dry before you go to bed! Take care when pressing; do a tiny test patch first and, if necessary, add extra layers under the shawl, such as blankets or towels to protect the surface underneath.
■ Use large glass-headed pins or quilting pins, as they're easier to handle and you're less likely to lose them in the lace.
■ If you are worried that little fingers might get caught in the lace, layer the shawl over a soft blanket.

CENTER

1st panel Make 47ch.

Row 1 1sc in 9th ch from hook, [6ch, skip 4ch, 1sc in next ch] 7 times, 3ch, 1dc in last ch.

Row 2 (RS) 4ch, [1 triple 3trcl in 6ch sp, 3ch, 1sc in next 6ch sp, 3ch] 3 times, 1 triple 3trcl in last 6ch sp, 3ch, skip 3ch, 1sc in next ch.

Row 3 7ch, [1sc in sp between clusters, 6ch] 7 times, 1sc in sp between clusters, 3ch, skip 3ch 1tr in next ch.

Rows 2 and 3 form the patt. Patt 61 more rows. 32 triple cluster fan patts have been completed.

Last row (WS) 5ch, [1sc in sp between clusters, 4ch] 7 times, 1sc in sp between clusters, 2ch, skip 3ch, 1dc in last ch. Make 3 more panels.

Join panels With RS facing, set two panels side by side. Join yarn in lower right-hand corner of left panel, 2ch, ss in 3rd ch of lower left-hand corner of right panel, 3ch, ss in corner sp of left panel, [3ch, ss in next sp of right panel, 3ch, ss in next sp of left panel] to last sp on left panel, 3ch, ss in last sp of right panel, 3ch, ss in top left corner sp, 2ch, ss in 3rd ch at top right corner. Fasten off. Join 3rd and 4th panels in the same way. Darn in all ends.

BORDER

With RS facing, join yarn in 2nd sp before top right corner sp.

Round 1 [3sc, 3ch, 3sc] in same sp as join, in next sp, and in corner sp, * [3sc, 3ch, 3sc] in each of next 7 sps along top edge, 2sc in corner sp, [1sc, 3ch, 1sc] in join between panels, 2sc in corner sp of next panel, rep from * along top edge, ending [3sc, 3ch, 3sc] in top left corner sp, [3sc, 3ch, 3sc] in each sp along side edge and in corner sp, rep from * along lower edge and side, ending ss in first sc. 31 3ch sps along each side and one 3ch sp at each corner.

Round 2 Ss in each of next 2sc, ss in first sp, 9ch, 1tr in same sp, ** 5ch, 1sc in next sp, 5ch, [1tr, 5ch] 3 times in corner sp, 1tr in same sp, * [5ch, 1sc in next sp, 5ch, [1tr, 5ch, 1tr] in foll sp, rep from * 14 more times, rep from ** 3 more times, ending 5ch, 1sc in next sp, 5ch, ss in 4th ch.

Round 3 [3sc, 3ch, 3sc] in same sp as join, ** 1sc in next sp, 3ch, 1sc in foll sp, [3sc, 3ch, 3sc] in each of next 3 sps, * 1sc in next sp, 3ch, 1sc in foll sp, [3sc, 3ch, 3sc] in next sp, rep from * 14 more times, rep from ** 3 more times, ending 1sc in next sp, 3ch, 1sc in last sp, ss in first sc.

Round 4 Ss in each of next 2sc, ss in first 3ch sp, 1sc in same sp, 5ch, [1tr, 5ch, 1tr] in next sp, ** 5ch, 1sc in next sp, 5ch, [1tr, 5ch] 3 times in corner sp, 1tr in same sp, * 5ch, 1sc in next sp, 5ch, [1tr, 5ch, 1tr] in next sp, rep from * 15 more times, rep from ** 3 more times, ending 5ch, ss in first sc.

Round 5 Ss in each of 4ch, 1sc in same sp as ss, [3sc, 3ch, 3sc] in foll sp, ** 1sc in next sp, 5ch, 1sc in next sp, [3sc, 3ch, 3sc] in each of next 3 sps, * 1sc in next sp, 5ch, 1sc in foll sp, [3sc, 3ch, 3sc] in next sp, rep from * 15 more times, rep from ** 3 more times, ending 5ch, ss in first sc.

Rounds 6 and 7 As Rounds 4 and 5, but rep from * 16 times.

Round 8 Ss each of next 2sc and 2ch, 1sc in first 3ch sp, [2ch, 1 triple 3tr cluster in next sp, 2ch, 1sc in foll sp] to end, omitting last sc, ss in first sc.

This exquisite shawl will be treasured forever.

Round 9 Ss in first ch, 3ch, 1dc in top of cluster, 3dc in next sp, [1dc, 3ch, 1dc] in next cluster, 3dc in next sp, ** 1dc in cluster, 1dc in each of next 2 sps, 1dc in cluster, 3dc in next sp, [2dc, 5ch, 2dc] in corner cluster, 3dc in next sp, * 1dc in next cluster, 1dc in each of next 2 sps, 1dc in cluster, 3dc in sp, [1dc, 3ch, 1dc] in next cluster, 3dc in sp, rep from * 17 more times, rep from ** 3 more times, ending ss in 3rd ch. Fasten off.

TO FINISH

Pin center out to a square; pin each loop out around the edges. Using a damp cloth, press then leave to dry. Remove pins; darn in ends.

This delicate little cropped cardigan is inspired
by the traditional crossover ballet top.

Sugar Plum Fairy Cardigan

This snug-fitting wrap-over top is worked in double crochet with a simple shell edging. It's very quick to make because each row gets you one centimeter nearer to finishing. Choose classic soft pink or match the cardigan to a favorite print dress.

ESTIMATED TIME TO COMPLETE
For the first size, 5 hours.

ABOUT THIS YARN
Debbie Bliss Cashmerino DK is a soft, smooth 55 percent merino-wool, 33 percent microfiber, and 12 percent cashmere yarn with 120 yd. (110 m) to a 50-g ball.

SIZES
To fit: age 3 to 6 months(**1 to 2**:2 to 3:**3 to 4**) years; **chest** 18(**20**:22:**24**) in. [46(**51**:56:**61**) cm]
Actual measurements: chest 20½(**22½**:24½:**26½**) in. [52.5(**57.5**:62.5:**67.5**) cm]; **length** 6¾(**7½**:9:**9¾**) in. [17(**19**:23:**25**) cm]; **sleeve** 7½(**8¼**:9¾:**10½**) in. [19(**21**:25:**27**) cm].
Figures in parentheses refer to larger sizes. One figure refers to all sizes.

YOU WILL NEED
- 3(**4**:5:**5**) x 50-g balls of Debbie Bliss Cashmerino DK in pink, shade 16
- E/4 (3.50-mm) crochet hook
- 2 buttons (optional)

GAUGE
16 sts and 10 rows to 4 in. (10 cm) over double crochet using E/4 (3.50-mm) hook. Change hook size if necessary to obtain this gauge.

ABBREVIATIONS
beg = beginning; **ch** = chain; **cont** = continue; **dc** = double crochet; **2dctog** = leaving last loop of each st on hook, work 2dc, yarn around hook and pull through 3 loops on hook; **inc** = increase; **RS** = right side; **sc** = single crochet; **ss** = slip stitch; **st(s)** = stitch(es); **WS** = wrong side; **yo** = yarn over hook; **[ ]** = work instructions in brackets as directed.

NOTE
The wrap is worked from the top down, so the lower edge is soft and flexible.

TIPS
■ Work the starting chain loosely; if necessary use a larger hook.
■ Buttons are safer for babies, but ties give a more authentic ballet look on the children's sizes. Choose the fastening you prefer.
■ Babies and children of the same age can be very different sizes, so check the measurements against a garment that you know fits the child well when choosing which size to make.
■ If you really can't bear to do a gauge sample, get started on the back and check the width after 7 rowsp. If your back measures 7¼(**8¼**:9¼:**10¼**) in. [18.5(**21**:23.5:**26**)cm] across, and 5 of the 7 rows measure 2 in. (5 cm), you're fine to continue.
■ When working the edging, work two surface chain into each row, with one chain extra on each front for the 2nd and 4th sizes.

BACK
Make 32(**36**:40:**44**) ch.
Row 1 (WS) 1dc in 4th ch from hook, [1dc in each ch] to end. 30(**34**:38:**42**) sts.
Row 2 1sc in first dc, 2ch, [1dc in each dc] to last st, 1dc in last ch.
Row 2 forms dc.
Cont in dc, work 7(**8**:9:**10**) more rows.
Shape armholes. Inc row. 1sc in first dc, 2ch, 1dc in same dc as sc, [1dc in each dc] to last st, 2dc in 2nd ch. Cont in dc, inc in this way at each end of next row. 34(**38**:42:**46**) sts. Fasten off.

Next row Make 4ch, 2dc in first dc, [1dc in each dc] to last st, 2dc in 2nd ch, make 6ch. 36(**40**:44:**48**) dc.

Next row 1dc in 4th ch from hook, 1dc in each of next 2ch, [1dc in each dc], 1dc in each of 4ch. 44(**48**:52:**56**) sts.

Cont in dc, work 4(**5**:8:**9**) rows. Fasten off.

RIGHT FRONT

Make 11(**12**:13:**14**)ch.

Work Row 1 as given for back.

9(**10**:11:**12**) sts.

Cont in dc as back, work 2 rows **.

Shape front. Row 4 (RS) 1sc in first dc, 2ch, [1dc in each dc] to last st, 2dc in 2nd ch.

Row 5 1sc in first dc, 2ch, 1dc in same dc as sc, [1dc in each dc] to last st, 1dc in 2nd ch.

Cont in dc, inc one st at front edge in same way as Rows 4 and 5 on next 4(**5**:6:**7**) rows. 15(**17**:19:**21**) sts.

Shape armhole Inc in same way as back at each end of next 2(**3**:2:**3**) rows. 19(**23**:23:**27**) sts.

1st and 3rd sizes Fasten off.

Next row (RS) Make 4ch, 2dc in first dc, [1dc in each dc] to last st, 2dc in 2nd ch.

Next row 1sc in first dc, 2ch, 1dc in same dc as sc, [1dc in each dc] to last dc, 1dc in each of next 4ch.

2nd and 4th sizes Do not turn at end of last row, make 6ch.

Next row (RS) 1dc in 4th ch from hook, 1dc in each of next 2ch, [1dc in each dc] to last st, 2dc in 2nd ch.

All sizes 26(**28**:30:**32**) sts. Cont in dc, inc at front edge on next 4(**5**:8:**9**) rows. 30(**33**:38:**41**) sts. Fasten off.

LEFT FRONT

Work as given for right front to **.

Shape front Cont in dc, inc 1 st at beg of next row and at this edge on next 5(**6**:7:**8**) rows. 15(**17**:19:**21**) sts.

Shape armhole Inc in same way as back at each end of next 3(**2**:3:**2**) rows. 19(**23**:23:**27**) sts.

1st and 3rd sizes Do not turn at end of last row, make 6ch.

Next row (RS) 1dc in 4th ch from hook, 1dc in each of next 2ch, [1dc in each dc] to last st, 2dc in 2nd ch.

2nd and 4th sizes Fasten off.

Next row (WS) Make 4ch, 2dc in first dc, [1dc in each dc] to last st, 2dc in 2nd ch.

Next row 1sc in first dc, 2ch, 1dc in same dc as sc, [1dc in each dc] to last dc, 1dc in each of next 4ch.

All sizes 26(**28**:30:**32**) sts. Cont in dc, inc at front edge on next 4(**5**:8:**9**) rows. 30(**33**:38:**41**) sts. Fasten off.

SLEEVES

Make 27(**29**:31:**33**) ch.

Work Row 1 as given for back.

25(**27**:29:**31**) sts.

Cont in dc as for back, work 2(**2**:4:**3**) rows, then inc one st at each end of next row in same way as back and at each end of 4(**5**:6:**7**) foll 3rd rows. 35(**39**:43:**47**) sts.

Inc at each end of next 3(**2**:1:**1**) rows. 41(**43**:45:**49**) sts.

Shape top. Row 1 Ss in each of first 4dc, 1sc in next dc, 2ch, 1dc in each dc to last 4 sts, turn. 33(**35**:37:**41**) sts.

Dec row 1sc in first dc, 1ch, [1dc in each dc] to last 2 sts, 2dctog. Cont in dc, work dec row 3(**4**:4:**5**) more times. 25(**25**:27:**29**) sts. Fasten off.

EDGING

Matching sts, join shoulders. With RS facing, join yarn at lower edge of right front. Inserting hook close to edge, work 34(**39**:46:**51**) surface chain up right front edge, 12(**14**:16:**18**) across back neck sts and 34(**39**:46:**51**) down left front edge.

Row 1 (WS) 1ch, 1sc into edge and over each surface chain. 80(**92**:108:**124**) sts.

Row 2 [Skip 1sc, 4dc in next sc, skip 1sc, ss in next sc] to end. Fasten off. Darn in ends.

TO FINISH

Press according to ball band. Set in sleeves. Taking 1 st in from each side, join side and sleeve seams. Either overlap fronts and sew on buttons, slipping buttons between stitches to fasten, or make ties and sew on ends of fronts.

TIES

Make 4ch, yo, insert hook in 4th ch from hook, yo and pull through, [yo and pull through] twice, inserting hook in 2 strands at top of previous st each time, cont working a dc chain in this way until tie measures 21½(**24**:25½:**28**) in. [55(**61**:65:**71**) cm]. Fasten off. Darn in ends.

These pretty little shoes
are perfect for baby girls.

Baby Mary Janes

All you need to know is chain, single crochet, and slip stitch to make these adorable little shoes. Each one is worked in the round, starting at the center of the sole, so there's no sewing up, apart from attaching the straps, and there are no seams to rub tiny feet.

ESTIMATED TIME TO COMPLETE
For the pair 3 hours.

ABOUT THIS YARN
Debbie Bliss Merino DK is a soft 100 percent merino-wool yarn with 120 yd. (110 m) to a 50-g ball.

SIZE
To fit: age 3 to 6 months
Actual measurement: along sole approximately 3½ in. (9 cm)

YOU WILL NEED
■ 1 x 50-g ball of Debbie Bliss Merino DK, in pink, shade 615
■ E/4 (3.50-mm) crochet hook
■ 2 small buttons

GAUGE
6 rounds of single crochet shaped as given for sole measure 3½ in. (9 cm) in length and 2⅛ in. (5.5 cm) wide using E/4 (3.50-mm) hook. Change hook size if necessary to obtain this size sole.

ABBREVIATIONS
ch = chain; **RS** = right side; **sc** = single crochet; **2sctog** = insert hook in first st, yo and pull through, insert hook in next st, yo and pull through, yo and pull through 3 loops on hook; foll = following; **ss** = slip st; **st(s)** = stitch(es); **yo** = yarn over hook; [ ] = work instructions in brackets as directed.

1sc in each of next 13sc, 2sc in foll sc, 1sc in each of next 4sc, 2sc in foll sc, 1sc in each of next 13sc, 2sc in foll sc, 1sc in last sc, ss in first sc. 40 sts.
Round 6 1ch, [1sc in each sc] to end, ss in first sc. Round 6 forms sc.
Upper Work 3 more rounds sc.
Shape front. Round 1 1ch, 1sc in each of first 16sc, [2sctog, 1sc in next sc] twice, 2sctog, 1sc in each of last 16sc, ss in first sc. 37 sts.
Round 2 1ch, 1sc in each of first 14sc, [2sctog] twice, 1sc in next sc, [2sctog] twice, 1sc in each of last 14sc, ss in first sc. 33 sts. Fasten off.
Strap Make 12ch. 1sc in 2nd ch from hook, [1sc in each ch] to end. Fasten off. Make second shoe and strap.

TO FINISH
Press according to ball band. Sew straps on inner edges of shoes. Sew on buttons to hold ends of straps in place.

SHOES
Sole Wrap yarn around finger to make a ring.
Round 1 (RS) 1ch, 8sc in ring, pull end to tighten ring, ss in first sc, make 6ch.
Round 2 2sc in 2nd ch from hook, 1sc in each of next 4ch, 1sc in each of next 2sc, 2sc in each of foll 4ch, 1sc in each of next 2sc, 1sc in base of next 4ch, 2sc in base of last ch, ss in first sc. 24 sts.

Round 3 1ch, 2sc in first sc, 1sc in each of next 9sc, 2sc in foll sc, 1sc in each of next 2sc, 2sc in foll sc, 1sc in each of next 9sc, 2sc in last sc, ss in first sc. 28 sts.
Round 4 1ch, 2sc in each of first 2sc, 1sc in each of next 9sc, 2sc in each of foll 2sc, 1sc in each of next 2sc, 2sc in each of foll 2 sc, 1sc in each of next 9sc, 2sc in each of last 2sc, ss in first sc. 36 sts.
Round 5 1ch, 1sc in first sc, 2sc in foll sc,

Enchanting Blue Elephant

This toy is worked all in very firm single crochet, mostly in the round, so the shape is very sculptural and the construction very strong. Add button eyes and fabric tongue and tusks as shown in the pictures if you're making the elephant for an older child or embroider the features if you're giving the toy to a baby or very young child.

ESTIMATED TIME TO COMPLETE

8 hours

ABOUT THIS YARN

Debbie Bliss Cotton DK is a firm, matte 100 percent cotton yarn with approximately 92 yd. (84 m) to a 50-g ball.

SIZE

Height (to shoulder) 6½ in. (16.5 cm)

YOU WILL NEED

- 3 x 50-g balls of Debbie Bliss Cotton DK in blue, shade 11
- D/3 (3.00-mm) crochet hook
- washable polyester fiberfill
- four 1½ x 1¼ in. (4 x 3 cm) ovals of soft leather, UltraSuede, or felt
- 2 small domed buttons and strong thread
- 1 pink and two cream 4 x 4 in. (10 x 10 cm) squares of fabric, matching sewing thread, and sharp needle (optional)

GAUGE

16 sts and 20 rows to 4 in. (10 cm) over single crochet worked in turning rounds using D/3 (3.00-mm) hook. Change hook size if necessary to obtain this gauge.

ABBREVIATIONS

beg = beginning; **ch** = chain; **cont** = continue; **inc** = increase; **RS** = right side; **sc** = single crochet; **2sctog** = insert hook in first st and pull loop through, insert hook in 2nd st and pull loop through, yarn around hook and pull through 3 loops on hook; **ss** = slip stitch; **st(s)** = stitch(es); **WS** = wrong side; **[ ]** = work instructions in brackets as directed.

NOTES

- The hook size and gauge given are tighter than would normally be used with this yarn, to make a firm fabric and a sculptural shape.
- If the elephant is for a baby or very small child, embroider the eyes, tongue and tusks with black, pink and cream yarn.

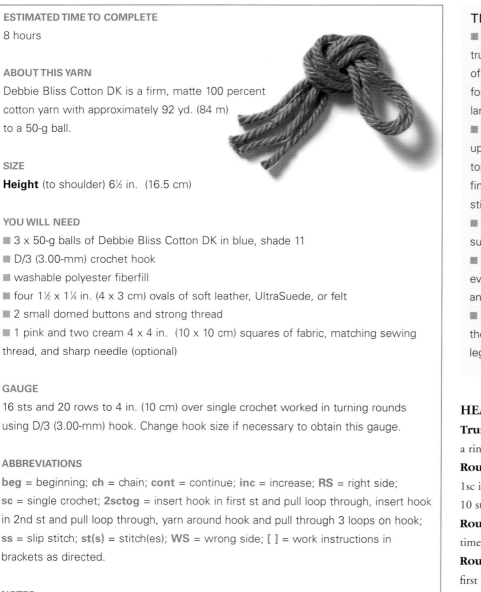

TIPS

- Don't put too much fiberfill in the trunk. Shape the face with small balls of fiberfill pushed into the cheeks and forehead before you fill the head with larger wads of fiberfill.
- If you want your elephant to stand up, pack the legs firmly to near the top, then pin the legs onto the body to find the best point of balance before stitching; add fiberfill if necessary.
- Go over each seam twice to make sure that the stitching is secure.
- As with all handmade toys, check every now and then for wear and tear and redo any stitching if necessary.
- Much of the elephant is worked in the round; join seams and sew on the legs and ears firmly.

HEAD AND BODY

Trunk Make 10ch, ss in first ch to form a ring.

Round 1 1ch, [working into back loop only, 1sc in each ch] to end, ss in first sc, turn. 10 sts.

Round 2 (RS) 1ch, 1sc in first sc, [2sctog] 4 times, 1sc in last sc, ss in first sc, turn. 6 sts.

Round 3 1ch, [1sc in each st] to end, ss in first sc, turn.

Round 3 forms sc. Turning each time, work 4 more rounds.

Round 8 1ch, 2sc in first sc, [1sc in each sc] to last sc, 2sc in last sc, ss in first sc, turn. 8 sts.

Cont in sc, turning each time, inc in this way at beg and end of next 3 RS rounds. 14 sts.

This cute little elephant will win
friends wherever he goes.

Next row (WS) 1ch, [1sc in each sc] to end, do not join in a round, turn.

Cont in sc, working in rows and turning after each row.

Face. **Row 1 (RS) 1ch, [2sc in each sc] to end. 28 sts.

Row 2 1ch, [1sc in each sc] to end.

Row 3 1ch, 1sc in each of first 9sc, 2sc in each of next 2sc, 1sc in each of foll 6sc, 2sc in each of next 2sc, 1sc in each of last 9sc. 32 sts **.

Row 4 1ch, 1sc in each of first 9sc, 2sc in each of next 4sc, 1sc in each of foll 6sc, 2sc in each of next 4sc, 1sc in each of last 9sc. 40 sts.

Cont in sc, work 2 rows.

Shape cheeks. Next row (RS) 1ch, 1sc in first sc, [2sctog] 3 times, 1sc in each of next 26sc, [2sctog] 3 times, 1sc in last sc. 34 sts.

Shape mouth. Next round With RS together, join first 3 and last 3 sts of previous row with sc, 1ch, [1sc in each sc] to end, ss in first sc after 1ch to join in a round, turn. 28 sts.

Turning each time, work 4 rounds sc.

Shape chest and neck. Round 1 (RS) 1ch, 2sc in each of first 3sc, 1sc in each of next 5sc, [2sctog] twice, 1sc in each of next 4sc, [2sctog] twice, 1sc in each of next 5sc, 2sc in each of last 3sc, ss in first sc, turn. 30 sts.

Round 2 1ch, 2sc in each of first 3sc, [1sc in each sc] to last 3sc, 2sc in each of last 3sc, ss in first sc, turn. 36 sts.

Round 3 1ch, [1sc in each of next 2sc, 2sc in foll sc] 3 times, [1sc in each sc] to last 9sc, [2sc in next sc, 1sc in each of foll 2sc] 3 times, ss in first sc, turn. 42 sts.

Make up and stuff head and body
Stitch end of trunk in a V shape and stuff trunk lightly. Join row ends of face. Fold corners of each cream square together to make a triangle, fold long edges together, then roll and stitch to form cone-shaped tusks. Insert points of tusks from WS through between stitches at each side of mouth; the bulk of the fabric will make it

impossible to pull through more than a small amount. Stitch in place and stuff around tusks, shaping face. Fold pink fabric in the same way but making a flatter tongue shape at the point, insert in mouth; and stitch to secure.

Stuff face Mark positions for eyes and ears. Knot shank of button in the center of a doubled length of strong thread. Using a large, sharp needle, thread one end, insert in right eye and bring out at right ear, thread the other end, insert in right eye and bring out at left ear. Do the same with the other button for the left eye, bringing ends out a few stitches apart. Pull ends to make eye sockets, firmly knot the threads together, darn in ends and trim.

Stuff head; stuff body before working the last few rounds of the bottom shaping.

Body Cont in sc and turning each time, work 11 rounds.

Shape tummy. Next round (RS) 1ch, 1sc in first sc, 2sc in each of next 3sc, [1sc in each sc] to last 4sc, 2sc in each of next 3sc, 1sc in last sc, ss in first sc, turn. 48 sts.

Cont in sc turning each time, work 9 rounds.

Shape bottom. Round 1 (RS) 1ch, 1sc in each of first 15sc, [2sctog, 1sc in each of next

2sc] 5 times, 1sc in each of last 13sc, ss in first sc, turn. 43 sts. Work 1 round.

Round 3 1ch, 1sc in each of first 3sc, [2sctog, 1sc in each of next 3sc] 8 times, ss in first sc, turn. 35 sts.

Round 4 1ch, 1sc in each of first 3sc, [2sctog, 1sc in each of next 2sc] 8 times, ss in first sc, turn. 27 sts.

Round 5 1ch, 1sc in each of first 3sc, [2sctog, 1sc in each of next 2sc] 6 times, ss in first sc, turn. 21 sts.

Round 6 1ch, 1sc in first sc, [2sctog] 10 times, ss in first sc, 11 sts.

Finish stuffing body.

Round 7 1ch, 1sc in first st, [2sctog] 5 times, ss in first sc, do not turn. 6 sts.

Tail. Next round 1ch, [2sctog] 3 times, ss in first st. 3 sts.

Cont working in a spiral for 6 more sc, work 2ch, fasten off. Add more strands of yarn through ch at end of tail; stitch and trim to form a small tassel.

LEGS

Front legs Make 18ch, ss in first ch to form a ring.

Turning each time, work 3 rounds sc. Insert oval footpads and stitch firmly to starting ch.

Shape foot. Next round (RS) 1ch, 1sc in each of first 5sc, [2sctog, 1sc in next sc] 3 times, 1sc in each of last 4sc, ss in first sc, turn. 15 sts ***.

Cont in sc and turning each time, work 13 rounds. Fasten off. Darn in ends.

Back legs Work as given for front legs to ***. Cont in sc turning each time, work 11 rounds. Fasten off.

EARS

Make 15ch.

Row 1 1sc in 2nd ch from hook, [1sc in each ch] to end. 14 sts.

Work as given for face from ** to **.

Work 1 more row sc. Fasten off.

TO FINISH

Stuff legs and sew in place on body. Sew on ears. Darn in ends.

Friendly Zebra

The zebra is worked in firm single crochet, mostly in the round. Using buttons for the eyes is optional; if you're making the toy for a baby, embroider the eyes instead. It's a really nice touch to make the zebra stand up on flexible legs reinforced with plastic-coated wire, but if you're making the toy for a baby, leave the wire out and stuff the legs firmly with fiberfill.

ESTIMATED TIME TO COMPLETE
For the zebra, 7 hours.

ABOUT THIS YARN
Rowan Handknit Cotton is a sturdy matte 100 percent cotton DK-weight yarn with approximately 93 yd. (85 m) to a 50-g ball.

SIZE
Height (to shoulder) 7½ in. (19 cm)

YOU WILL NEED
■ 1 x 50-g ball of Rowan Handknit Cotton in each of black, shade 252 (A), and ecru, shade 251 (B)
■ D/3 (3.00-mm) crochet hook
■ washable polyester fiberfill
■ pink embroidery floss
■ 2 small buttons and strong thread (optional)
■ 4 x 9½-in. (24-cm) lengths of plastic-coated wire (optional)

GAUGE
16 sts and 20 rows to 4 in. (10 cm) over single-crochet stripe patt worked in turning rounds using D/3 (3.00-mm) hook. Change hook size if necessary to obtain this gauge.

ABBREVIATIONS
ch = chain; **cont** = continue; **patt** = pattern; **RS** = right side; **sc** = single crochet; **2sctog** = insert hook in first st and pull loop through, insert hook in 2nd st and pull loop through, yarn over hook and pull through 3 loops on hook; **ss** = slip stitch; **st(s)** = stitch(es); **WS** = wrong side; [ ] = work instructions in brackets as directed.

NOTES
■ The hook size and gauge given are tighter than would usually be used with this yarn to make a firm fabric and a sculptural shape.
■ The construction is strong but make sure that you join seams and sew on the legs, ears, tail, and mane firmly.
■ If you are making the zebra for a baby or very small child, embroider the eyes.

TIPS
■ Leave a long end when making the ring at the start of the head. Pinch the first few rounds together and use the end to stitch the rounds into a triangular mouth shape. Do this while you can still get your fingers inside!
■ As with all handmade toys, check every now and then for wear and tear, and redo any stitching if necessary.

HEAD AND BODY
Shape nose Using A, wind yarn around finger to form a ring. Pull end to tighten ring.
Round 1 (RS) 1ch, 9sc in ring, ss in first sc, turn. 9 sts.
Round 2 1ch, [1sc in each sc] to end, ss in first sc, turn.
Round 3 1ch, 2sc in first sc, [1sc in each of next 2sc, 3sc in next sc] twice, 1sc in each of next 2sc, 1sc in same sc as first 2sc, ss in first sc, turn. 15 sts.

Round 4 1ch, [1sc in each sc] to end, ss in first sc, turn.

Round 4 forms sc.

Round 5 1ch, 1sc in each of first 5sc, [4sc in next sc, 1sc in each of next 4sc] twice, ss in first sc, turn. 21 sts.

Work 1 round sc, turn.

Change to B. Work 2 rounds sc, turning at the end of each round.

Change to A. Work 2 rounds sc, turning at the end of each round.

The last 4 rows form the stripe patt.

Cont in sc stripe patt, work 3 rows.

Shape head. Round 1 (WS) 1ch, 1sc in each of first 8sc, 2sc in each of next 6sc, 1sc in each of last 7sc, ss in first sc, turn. 27 sts.

Work 1 round.

Round 3 1ch, 1sc in each of first 12sc, 2sc in each of next 4sc, 1sc in each of last 11sc, ss in first sc, turn. 31 sts.

Work 1 round sc. Fasten off.

With WS facing, join A in 4th sc to left of join in previous row.

** **NECK.**

Row 1 1ch, 1sc in same place as join, 1sc in each of next 23sc, turn. Cont changing colors for stripe patt.

Row 2 1ch, skip first sc, 1sc in each of next 22sc, turn.

Row 3 1ch, skip first sc, 1sc in each of next 20sc, turn.

Row 4 1ch, skip first sc, 1sc in each of next 18sc, turn.

Row 5 1ch, skip first sc, 1sc in each of next 16sc, turn.

Row 6 1ch, skip first sc, 1sc in each of next 14sc, turn.

Row 7 1ch, skip first sc, 1sc in each of next 12sc, turn.

Row 8 1ch, skip first sc, 1sc in each of next 10sc, turn.

Row 9 1ch, skip first sc, 1sc in each of next 8sc, turn.

Row 10 1ch, skip first sc, 1sc in each of next 6sc, turn.

Rows 11 and 12 1ch, 1sc in each sc. 6 sts.

Row 13 1ch, 2sc in first sc, 1sc in next sc, 2sc in each of next 2sc, 1sc in foll sc, 2sc in

last sc. 10 sts. Work 1 row.

Row 15 1ch, 2sc in first sc, 1sc in each of next 3sc, 2sc in each of foll 2sc, 1sc in each of next 3sc, 2sc in last sc. 14 sts.

Work 1 row.

Row 17 1ch, 2sc in first sc, 1sc in each of next 5sc, 2sc in each of foll 2sc, 1sc in each of next 5sc, 2sc in last sc. 18 sts.

Work 1 row.

Row 19 1ch, 2sc in first sc, 1sc in each of next 7sc, 2sc in each of foll 2sc, 1sc in each of next 7sc, 2sc in last sc. 22 sts.

Work 1 row. Fasten off.

With WS facing, join A in center st at front neck.

Joining round (WS) 1ch, 1sc in same place as join, 1sc in each of next 3sc across front neck, 1sc in corner, 1sc in each of 22sc around back neck, 1sc in front neck corner, 1sc in each of last 3sc across front neck, ss in first sc, turn. 31 sts **.

Cont in stripe patt, work 2 more rounds sc.

Next round (RS) 1ch, 1sc in each of next 14sc, 2sc in next sc, 1sc in each of next 14sc, 2sctog, ss in first sc. 31 sts. Fasten off.

Shape chest Count back 12 sts from join and join A in this 12th st. Work as given for neck from ** to **, joining in at center back neck before working Joining round and reading back for front on Joining round. Using pink floss, embroider tongue; using B, embroider teeth. Fasten off.

Body Join yarn at opposite side of round so joins will be under tummy. Cont in sc stripe patt, work 19 more rounds.

Shape bottom. Round 1 (WS) 1ch, 1sc in first sc, [2sctog] twice, [1sc in each sc] to last 4sc, [2sctog] twice, ss in first sc. 27 sts.

Work 1 round.

Round 3 1ch, 1sc in first sc, [2sctog, 1sc in next st] 8 times, 2sctog, ss in first sc, turn. 18 sts.

Work 1 round.

Round 5 1ch, [2sctog] 9 times, ss in first st. 9 sts. Leaving a long end, fasten off.

LEGS

Using A, wrap yarn around finger to form a

ring. Pull end to tighten ring.

Round 1 (RS) 1ch, 8sc in ring, ss in first sc, turn. 8 sts.

Round 2 1ch, 2sc in each of first 4sc, 1sc in each of last 4sc, ss in first sc, turn. 12 sts.

Round 3 1ch, 1sc in each sc, ss in first sc, turn.

Round 4 1ch, [2sctog] 4 times, 1sc in each of next 4sc, ss in first sc, turn. 8 sts.

Change to B. Cont in sc stripe patt, work 15 rounds.

Next round (WS) 1ch, 2sc in first sc, [1sc in next sc, 2sc in foll sc] 3 times, 1sc in last sc, ss in first sc, turn. 12 sts.

Cont in sc stripe patt, work 4 rounds.

Fasten off. Darn in ends.

EARS

Using A, make 5ch.

Row 1 1sc in 2nd ch from hook, [1sc in each ch] to end. 4 sts.

Cont in sc, work 6 rows.

Next row 1ch, [2sctog] twice. 2 sts.

Next row 1ch, 2sctog. Fasten off.

TO FINISH

Using a blunt-pointed needle, thread end through sts of last round of body. Draw up and secure. Press first 3 to 4 rounds at nose inward at an angle, pinch sides together, and stitch with A to form a mouth shape as shown in the picture. Join neck seams and one chest seam.

Stuff head and body. Join remaining chest seam. Using strong thread doubled, stitch one eye in place bringing thread out at opposite ear position. Secure ends. Repeat for second eye. Sew ears on, hiding eye thread ends. Stuff legs, inserting plastic-coated wire if desired—fold in half and wrap in stuffing with ends turned over to avoid sharp wires protruding. Sew legs on body.

Mane Using A, make 11 tassels each 1¼ in. (3 cm) long. Work a row of surface chain down back neck and sew tassels on chain and trim.

Tail Using A, make a tassel approximately 3½ in. (9 cm) long. Sew in place and trim.

This adorable zebra has
lots of character.

Candy-Striped Jacket

Easy-to-work single crochet creates a waffle-like surface that looks very effective in a simple stripe pattern. The construction is simple too; each half of the jacket is worked from the cuff to the center, so when you've worked the first half, your fingers will "know" what to do for the second. The stripes will also help keep track when counting rows.

ESTIMATED TIME TO COMPLETE
For the 2nd-size jacket, 13 hours.

ABOUT THIS YARN
Debbie Bliss Baby Cashmerino is lighter than sport-weight but more substantial than most fingering-weight yarns. It's a mix of 55 percent merino wool, 33 percent microfiber, and 12 percent cashmere with 137 yd. (125 m) to a 50-g ball.

SIZES
To fit: age 3(**6**:12) months; **chest** 16(**18**:20) in. [41(**46**:51) cm]; height 25(**28¼**:31½) in. [64(**72**:80) cm]
Actual measurements: chest 18(**23½**:28¾) in. [46(**60**:73) cm]; **length** 8½(**10¼**:12¼) in. [22(**26**:31.5) cm]; **sleeve** (with cuff turned back) 5½(**6½**:8½) in. [14(**16.5**:21.5) cm]
Figures in parentheses refer to larger sizes. One figure refers to all sizes.

YOU WILL NEED
■ 3(**3**:4) x 50-g balls of Debbie Bliss Baby Cashmerino, in cream, shade 101 (A)
■ 1(**2**:3) x 50-g balls same in duck egg, shade 202 (B)
■ D/3 (3.00-mm) crochet hook
■ 4 buttons
■ blunt-pointed needle

GAUGE
19 sts and 24 rows to 4 in. (10 cm) over single crochet using D/3 (3.00-mm) hook. Change hook size if necessary to obtain this gauge.

ABBREVIATIONS
ch = chain; **cont** = continue; **dec** = decrease; **foll** = following; **inc** = increase; **patt** = pattern; **RS** = right side; **sc** = single crochet; **2sctog** = insert hook in next st and pull loop through, insert hook in foll st and pull loop through, yo and pull through 3 loops on hook; **ss** = slip stitch; **st(s)** = stitch(es); **WS** = wrong side; **yo** = yarn over hook; **[ ]** = work instructions in brackets as directed.

NOTE
The jacket is worked in two halves and joined at the center back.

TIPS
■ It really helps to put markers at each end of the increase rows for the sleeve so you can see at a glance how many increases you have done.
■ Make sure you work the chain for the side seam loosely or it will pull up. If necessary, use a hook one or two sizes larger.
■ It's okay to carry the A yarn up over the two row ends of the stripe in B, but the B yarn shows up against the four rows in A, so the edge looks better if you cut the B yarn and darn in the ends.
■ The back seam will be flatter if you sew the pieces together. You could join the seam with crochet, but it will make a ridge.
■ If you want to make matching bootees, follow the instructions for the Striped Bootees on page 128, working in stripes of 2 rows A, 2 rows B. The 2nd-size jacket takes almost all of the cream yarn, so if you want to make matching bootees in this size, you'll need an extra ball of A.
■ If you want to make the jacket in one color, you'll need approximately 4(**5**:6) x 50-g balls of Debbie Bliss Baby Cashmerino.
■ Instructions are given for working buttonholes for a girl in the right front and for a boy in the left front. Omit whichever set of buttonholes is not needed.

This cute little jacket is just
right for a boy or a girl.

RIGHT HALF

Cuff Using A, make 33(**37**:43)ch.

Row 1 1sc in 2nd ch from hook, 1sc in each ch to end. 32(**36**:42) sts.

Row 2 1ch, 1sc in each sc to end.

Row 2 forms single crochet.

Cont in A, work 7(**9**:9) more rows.

Sleeve Cont in sc, work 2 rows B, 4 rows A.

These 6 rows form the stripe patt.

Cont in sc stripe patt, work 2 more rows, ending with a 2nd row in B.

Inc row (RS) Using A, 1ch, 2sc in first sc, [1sc in each sc] to last sc, 2sc in last sc.

Cont in sc stripe patt, inc in this way at each end of 6(**7**:6) foll 4th rows.

3rd size only Inc at each end of 2 foll 6th rows.

All sizes 46(**52**:60) sts.

Patt 1(**3**:7) rows, ending with a 2nd row in A, do not turn at end of last row, make 20(**25**:31)ch loosely.

Back and front. Next row 1sc in 2nd ch from hook, 1sc in each of next 18(**23**:29)ch, 1sc in each of 46(**52**:60)sc across sleeve, 1sc in base of 19(**24**:30)ch. 84(**100**:120) sts.

Cont in sc stripe patt, work 17(**23**:29) rows, ending with a 2nd row in A **.

Front neck. Row 1 (RS) 1ch, 1sc in each of 36(**44**:53)sc, turn and leave 48(**56**:67)sc.

Row 2 2sctog, 1sc in each sc to end.

Row 3 1ch, 1sc in each sc to last 2 sc, 2sctog. Cont in patt, dec in same way as Rows 2 and 3 on next 1(**3**:4) rows. 33(**39**:47) sts.

Boy's jacket Patt 8(**8**:9) rows. Fasten off.

Girl's jacket Patt 5(**5**:6) rows.

Buttonhole row (WS) 1ch, 1sc in first sc, [2ch, skip 2sc, 1sc in each of next 6(**7**:9)sc] 3 times, 2ch, skip 2sc, 1sc in each of last 6(**9**:11)sc.

Next row 1ch, 1sc in each sc to 2ch sp, [2sc in 2ch sp, 1sc in each of next 6(**7**:9)sc] 3 times, 2sc in 2ch sp, 1sc in last sc. Patt 1 row. Fasten off.

Back neck With RS facing, join A in 8th(**8th**:9th)sc from first row of front neck.

Row 1 1ch, 1sc in same place as join, 1sc in

each sc to end. 41(**49**:59) sts.

Patt 9(**11**:13) more rows. Fasten off.

LEFT HALF

Work as given for right half to **.

Back neck. Row 1 (RS) 1ch, 1sc in each of next 41(**49**:59)sc, turn and leave 43(**51**:61)sc. Patt 9(**11**:13) more rows. Fasten off.

Front neck With RS facing, join yarn in 8th(**8th**:9th)sc from Row 1 of back neck.

Row 1 1ch, 1sc in each sc to end. 36(**44**:53) sc.

Cont in patt, dec at neck edge in same way as right front neck on next 3(**5**:6) rows. 32(**39**:47) sts.

Girl's jacket Patt 8(**8**:9) rows. Fasten off.

Boy's jacket Patt 5(**5**:6) rows.

Buttonhole row (WS) 1ch, 1sc in each of next 6(**9**:11)sc, [2ch, skip 2sc, 1sc in each of next 6(**7**:9)sc] 3 times, 2ch, skip 2sc, 1sc in last sc.

Next row 1ch, 1sc in first sc, [2sc in 2ch sp, 1sc in each of next 6(**7**:9)sc] 3 times, 2sc in 2ch sp, 1sc in each of last 6(**9**:11)sc.

Patt 1 row. Fasten off. Darn in ends.

COLLAR

Join back seam. With RS facing, join A in 5th row end from right front edge.

Row 1 1ch, 8(**10**:12)sc in row ends and 1sc in each of 7(**7**:8)sc up right front neck, 20(**24**:28)sc across back neck, 1sc in each of 7(**7**:8)sc and 8(**10**:12)sc in row ends down left front neck, ending in 5th row end from left front edge. 50(**58**:68) sts. Work 1 row sc.

Inc row 1ch, 1sc in first sc, * [2sc in next sc, 1sc in each of foll 2sc] 4 times, 2sc in next sc *, 1sc in each of foll 22(**30**:40)sc, rep from * to *, 1sc in last sc. 60(**68**:78) sc. Work 8(**8**:10) rows sc. Fasten off. Darn in ends.

EDGING

With RS facing, join B at center back.

Round 1 Work surface chain as close to the edge as possible in row ends and sts around all edges, turning the chain to the other side for the collar, ss in first ch.

Round 2 1ch, [1sc over each ch] to end, ss in first sc. Fasten off.

TO FINISH

Darn in ends. Press according to ball band. Join sleeve seams. Fold cuff back and work edging in B. Sew on buttons.

Baby Blanket

Sturdy enough to use as a play mat or a stroller cover but soft enough to cuddle up with in a crib, the simple, solid squares that make up this practical little blanket are worked mostly in doubles, with triples at the corners, then finished with a border in single crochet. And you'll enjoy the trick that makes working with color in the round neat and easy to do.

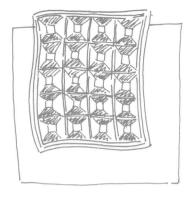

ESTIMATED TIME TO COMPLETE
Each square 40 minutes; blanket 17 hours.

ABOUT THIS YARN
Debbie Bliss Cotton DK is a 100 percent cotton yarn with 92 yd. (84 m) to a 50-g ball.

SIZE
Width 24 in. (61 cm); **length** 29 ½ in. (75 cm)

YOU WILL NEED
■ 4 x 50-g balls of Debbie Bliss Cotton DK in cream, shade 002 (A)
■ 4 x 50-g balls of same in duck egg, shade 009 (B)
■ 3 x 50-g balls of same in taupe, shade 019 (C)
■ F/5 (4.00-mm) crochet hook

GAUGE
Each 5-round square measures 5¼ x 5¼ in. (13 x 13 cm) using F/5 (4.00-mm) hook. Change hook size if necessary to obtain this size square.

ABBREVIATIONS
dc = double crochet; **foll** = following; **RS** = right side; **sc** = single crochet; **ss** = slip stitch; **st(s)** = stitch(es); **tr** = triple; **[ ]** = work instructions in brackets as directed.

NOTES
■ Use the yarn from the center of the ball and the yarn from the outside for opposite color sections or use a separate ball for each section.
■ When changing colors, always pull through the last loop of the last stitch of the previous section with the new color.
■ When changing colors on Rounds 4 and 5, say from B to C, work to the last pull-through of the last stitch in B, bring the C yarn back to the start of the section, laying it loosely along the top of the stitches and (except for the first color change of the round) allowing enough extra for the height of the first stitch. Pull through the last stitch in B with C, then catch the strand at the back in with the first stitch and work over the strand as you work into the stitches for that section.

TIPS
■ Make the last of the chain at the beginning of a round loosely; this will make it easier to work into it when joining the round.
■ For a neater finish to the squares, don't fasten off in the usual way; instead, pull up the chain from the last stitch until it's about 3 in. (8 cm) long, cut the chain in the center, remove the yarn from the ball, tighten the end, and darn it in.
■ When working the joining single crochet, hold the squares with wrong sides together, square from below in front and square from above behind, with the top edge slightly protruding; insert hook from RS into square in front and WS into square behind.
■ Take care not to turn the squares over when you are working the horizontal joins.

PATCHWORK SQUARE
Using A, wind yarn around finger to make a ring.
Round 1 3ch, 11 dc in ring, pull end to close ring, ss in 3rd ch. 12 sts.
Round 2 4ch, 2dc in same place a ss, * 1dc in next dc, [2dc, 1tr] in foll dc, [1tr, 2dc] in next dc, rep from * two more times, 1dc in next dc, [2dc, 1tr] in foll dc, change to B to pull through last loop of last st and ss in 4th ch.

Round 3 Using B work 4ch, 2dc in same place as ss, 1dc in each of next 5dc, [2dc, 1tr] in next tr, using C work * [1tr, 2dc] in foll tr, 1dc in each of next 5dc, [2dc, 1tr] in last tr *, using B, rep from * to *, using C, rep from * to *, pull through last st and ss in 4th ch with B.

Round 4 Using B work 4ch, 1dc in same place as ss, 1dc in each of next 9dc, [1dc, 1tr] in next tr, using C work * [1tr, 1dc] in foll tr, 1dc in each of next 9dc, [1dc, 1tr] in last tr *, using B, rep from * to *, using C, rep from * to *, pull through last st and ss in 4th ch with B.

Round 5 Using B work 4ch, 2dc in same place as ss, 1dc in each of next 11dc, [2dc, 1tr] in next tr, using C work * [1tr, 2dc] in

foll tr, 1dc in each of next 11dc, [2dc, 1tr] in last tr *, using B, rep from * to *, using C, rep from * to *. Fasten off.
Make 20 squares.

JOIN SQUARES
Lay squares down in a rectangle that is 4 squares wide by 5 squares long with sections in B at each side and sections in C at top and bottom. Work the horizontal joins first.

1st line Join A with a sc in first st in C at lower right corner of top right square, * 1sc in st in C at top right corner of square below, [1sc in next st of first square, 1sc in next st of 2nd square] 16 times, 3ch, 1sc in corner of next square above, rep from * to join remaining pairs of squares, ending with 1sc in corner stitch of last square.
Join 2nd line to 3rd, 3rd line to 4th and 4th line to 5th in the same way.
Work vertical joins in the same way, working 1ch, 1sc over 3ch, 1ch between corners of each pair of squares.

BORDER
With RS facing, join A in first st in B at lower right corner.

Round 1 1ch, 2sc in same st as join, * 1sc in each of next 16 sts, [2sc in join, 1sc in each of next 17 sts] 3 times, 2sc in join, 1sc in each of next 16 sts, 2sc in last st of this side, 2sc in first st of next side; work instructions in square brackets twice along top, 3 times down left side and twice along lower edge, rep from * to end, omitting last 2sc, ss in first sc. 342 sts.

Round 2 1ch, 2sc in first sc, * [1sc in each sc] to last st before corner, 2sc in each of next 2sc, rep from * to end, omitting last 2sc, ss in first sc. 350 sts.

Cont in sc increasing at corners in this way on every round, work 1 more round A and 3 rounds B. Fasten off. Darn in ends.

This beautiful blanket is inspired by a traditional patchwork block that looks like cotton spools or bows.

Charming Blue Beret

This sweet little hat is worked entirely in single crochet. It's really easy to do because you simply skip stitches to shape the top and there's just one seam to join. The combination of a firm stitch pattern, a firm gauge, and pure cotton yarn makes a three-dimensional, almost sculptural shape even though the hat is worked in rows.

ESTIMATED TIME TO COMPLETE
For the first-size beret, 3 hours.

ABOUT THIS YARN
Debbie Bliss Cotton DK is a 100 percent cotton yarn.
It has 92 yd. (84 m) to a 50-g ball.

SIZES
To fit: age 6 to 12 months(**2 to 3**:4 to 5) years
**Actual measurement: circumference around
head** 16¾(**18**:19½) in. [42(**46**:49) cm];
Figures in parentheses refer to larger sizes. One figure refers to all sizes.

YOU WILL NEED
- 2(**3**:3) x 50-g balls of Debbie Bliss Cotton DK in blue, shade 011
- E/4 (3.50-mm) crochet hook

GAUGE
17 sts and 20 rows to 4 in. (10 cm) over single crochet using E/4 (3.50-mm) hook.
Change hook size if necessary to obtain this gauge.

ABBREVIATIONS
ch = chain; **cont** = continue; **dec** = decrease; **foll** = following; **inc** = increase;
RS = right side; **sc** = single crochet; **ss** = slip stitch; **st(s)** = stitch(es); **WS** = wrong
side; **[ ]** = work instructions in brackets as directed.

TIPS
- Always join in a new ball of yarn at a side edge, not within a row.
- Lengths of contrast yarn woven backward and forward between the rows to mark the panels will help you see where to decrease.

Work 1 row.
2nd dec row (RS) 1ch, 1sc in first sc, [skip 1sc, 1sc in each of next 11(**12**:13)sc, skip 1sc, 1sc in next sc] 6 times.
73(**79**:85) sts.
Work 1 row.
3rd dec row (RS) 1ch, 1sc in first sc, [skip 1sc, 1sc in each of next 9(**10**:11)sc, skip 1sc, 1sc in next sc] 6 times.
61(**67**:73) sts.
Cont in sc, dec by skipping 1 st at each side of each panel in same way as before on next 4(**4**:5) RS rows. 13(**19**:13) sts. Work 1 row.
1st and 3rd sizes. Next row (RS) 1ch, 1sc in first sc, [skip 1sc, 1sc in next sc] 6 times.
2nd size only. Next row (RS) 1ch, 1sc in first sc, [skip 2sc, 1sc in next sc] 6 times.
All sizes 7 sts. Work 1 row.
Next row (RS) 1ch, 1sc in first sc, [skip 1sc, 1sc in next sc] 3 times. 4 sts.
Join in a round with ss in first sc, and working around 4sc in a spiral, work 12sc. Fasten off. Darn in ends.

TO FINISH

Join back seam, reversing seam for 5 rows at lower edge for turn-back brim.

HAT

Make 74(**80**:86)ch.
Row 1 (RS) 1sc in 2nd ch from hook, [1sc in each ch] to end. 73(**79**:85) sts.
Row 2 1ch, [1sc in each sc] to end.
2nd row forms sc. Work 9(**11**:13) more rows.
1st inc row (WS) 1ch, 1sc in first sc, [2sc in next sc, 1sc in each of foll 9(**10**:11)sc, 2sc in next sc, 1sc in foll sc] 6 times.
85(**91**:97) sts.

Work 3 rows sc.
2nd inc row (WS) 1ch, 1sc in first sc, [2sc in next sc, 1sc in each of foll 11(**12**:13)sc, 2sc in next sc, 1sc in foll sc] 6 times.
97(**103**:109) sts.
Work 6(**8**:10) rows sc.
1st dec row (RS) 1ch, 1sc in first sc, [skip 1sc, 1sc in each of next 13(**14**:15)sc, skip 1sc, 1sc in next sc] 6 times.
85(**91**:97) sts.

Shapelier than your average beret, this hat is sure to catch lots of attention.

Indigo-Dye Coat

This duffel coat is worked all in half-double crochet with single crochet seams and crab-stitch edging. The nice thing about half-double is that it grows fast but is less open than a double crochet fabric, making it ideal for this roomy little duffel coat. And because it's in indigo-dyed yarn, which fades with time, this coat gets better and better as it is washed and worn.

ESTIMATED TIME TO COMPLETE

For the 2nd-size duffel, 24 hours.

ABOUT THIS YARN

Elle True Blue is 100 percent cotton sport-weight yarn that's dyed with indigo, so it shrinks the first time it is washed and fades with wear. It has 118 yd. (108 m) to a 50-g ball.

SIZES

To fit: age 1(**3**:5) years; **chest** 20(**22**:24) in. [51(**56**:61) cm]
Actual measurements after washing: chest 29(**32**:34½) in. [74(**81**:87.5) cm]; **length** 15(**17**:18¼) in. [38.5(**43.5**:46.5) cm]; **sleeve** (with cuff turned back) 7½(**9½**:11¼) in. [19.5(**24**:29) cm]. Figures in parentheses refer to larger sizes. One figure refers to all sizes.

YOU WILL NEED

- 8(**10**:12) x 50-g balls of Elle True Blue DK in Denim, shade 112
- E/4 (3.50-mm) crochet hook
- 4 ring and toggle fastenings
- 48 in. (122 cm) of ⅛-in. (3-mm) wide suede

GAUGE

18 sts and 12 rows to 4 in. (10 cm) over half-double crochet, before washing, using E/4 (3.50-mm) hook. Change hook size if necessary to obtain this gauge.

ABBREVIATIONS

ch = chain; **cont** = continue; **dec** = decrease; **hdc** = half-double crochet; **2hdctog** = [yo, insert hook in next st and pull loop through] twice, yo and pull through all loops on hook; **3hdctog** = [yo, insert hook in next st and pull loop through] 3 times, yo and pull through all loops on hook; **RS** = right side; **sc** = single crochet; **st(s)** = stitch(es); **WS** = wrong side; **yo** = yarn over hook; **[ ]** = work instructions in brackets as directed.

NOTE

Elle True Blue shrinks by 5 percent in length after the first wash and fades gradually with every wash. The instructions take this into account.

TIPS

- Do not count the 2 chain at the start of a row as a stitch.
- Work the starting chain loosely. If necessary, use a larger hook.
- Do not join in a new ball of yarn within a row or at the front edges; always join at a side edge so the ends can be darned into the seam.
- Don't darn in ends before washing the garment; use the shrunk yarn to sew up.
- Because indigo is a surface dye, the center of the yarn frays into little white tassels at the ends when washed, so tie a tight knot right at the end of each yarn end, then fold the yarn over and tie in a loose slip knot to keep it out of the way while the garment is washed.
- Baste the fronts together before washing.
- Although the ball band recommends hand washing, you can wash the duffel coat in a machine; just use a gentle-wash action and make sure that the water temperature matches that given on the ball band. To preserve the color on subsequent washings, turn the coat inside out.
- You could make your own ring and toggle fastenings from brass curtain rings and wood, plastic, or horn toggles, or you could use traditional toggles and loops.
- You could use leather, cotton cord, or braid instead of narrow suede for the fastenings.

Made-to-fade
denim yarn
makes this coat
a favorite casual
classic.

BACK

Make 69(**75**:81)ch.

Row 1 (WS) 1hdc in 3rd ch from hook, [1hdc in each ch] to end. 67(**73**:79) sts.

Row 2 2ch, [1hdc in each hdc] to end. Row 2 forms hdc. Cont in hdc, work 47(**53**:57) more rows. Fasten off.

LEFT FRONT

Make 40(**43**:46)ch.

Row 1 (WS) Work as given for Row 1 of back. 38(**41**:44) sts.

Cont in hdc as given for back, work 42(**46**:48) more rows **.

Shape neck. Next row (RS) 2ch, 1hdc in each of next 21(**24**:27)hdc, 3hdctog, 1hdc in next hdc, turn, leave 13hdc. 23(**26**:29) sts. Mark 6th st from front edge. Work 1 row.

Dec row (RS) 2ch, [1hdc in each hdc] to last 4hdc, 3hdctog, 1hdc in last hdc.

Cont in hdc, dec in this way at end of next 1(**2**:3) RS rows. 19(**20**:21) sts.

Work 1 row. Fasten off.

RIGHT FRONT

Work as left front to **. Fasten off.

Shape neck. Next row (RS) Leave 13hdc, join yarn in next hdc, 2ch, 1hdc in same hdc as join, 3hdctog, [1hdc in each hdc] to end. 23(**26**:29) sts.

Mark 6th st from front edge. Work 1 row.

Dec row (RS) 2ch, 1hdc in first hdc, 3hdctog, [1hdc in each hdc] to end.

Cont in hdc, dec in this way at beg of next 1(**2**:3) RS rows. 19(**20**:21) sts.

Work 1 row. Fasten off.

SLEEVES

Make 36(**38**:42)ch.

Row 1 (WS) Work as given for Row 1 of back. 34(**36**:40) sts.

Cont in hdc as back, work 5(**5**:7) rows.

Inc row 2ch, 1hdc in first hdc, 2hdc in next hdc, [1hdc in each hdc] to last 2hdc, 2hdc in next hdc, 1hdc in last hdc.

Cont in hdc, inc in this way at each end of 6(**8**:9) foll 3rd rows. 48(**54**:60) sts.

Work 3(**3**:4) rows. Fasten off.

HOOD

With WS together and fronts facing, join shoulders with a row of sc. Fasten off. Make 93(**103**:113)ch.

Row 1 (WS) Work as given for Row 1 of back. 91(**101**:111) sts.

Cont in hdc as back, work 2 rows.

Dec row (RS) 2ch, 2hdctog, [1hdc in each hdc] to last 2 hdc, 2hdctog.

Cont in hdc, dec in this way at each end of next 4(**5**:6) RS rows. 81(**89**:97) sts. Work 5 rows.

1st side of back. Next row (RS) 2ch, 1hdc in each of next 30(**32**:34)hdc, turn.

Cont in hdc until hood reaches from markers to center back neck. Fasten off.

2nd side of back With RS facing, leave center 21(**25**:29)hdc, join yarn in next hdc.

Next row 2ch, 1hdc in same place as join, [1hdc in each hdc] to end. 30(**32**:34) sts. Complete to match first side. Fasten off.

POCKETS

(Make 2) Make 16(**18**:20)ch. Work Row 1 as given for back. 14(**16**:18) sts.

Cont in hdc as back, work 8(**9**:10) rows. Work 1 row crab st. Fasten off.

TO FINISH

With WS together and fronts facing, join back seam of hood with sc, then join row ends to sts left free at top of hood. Pin center back seam of hood to center back neck. Pin hood edge at intervals around neck edge between markers, easing to fit; join with sc. Work crab stitch along each front edge from hem to hood. Place markers 5¼ (**6**:6¾) in. [13.5(**15**:17) cm] down from shoulders on back and fronts. Join sleeves between markers with sc. Sew on pockets. Wash and dry duffel. Sew side and sleeve seams, reversing seam at cuff for 1 in. (2.5 cm). Turn back cuffs. Darn in ends. Cut the narrow suede into 8 equal lengths, loop through rings and thread through toggles, knot ends; sew on fronts.

Jester's Hat

Use up leftover yarn to make this colorful variation on a simple bag hat. It's all in single crochet, so it's easy to do. To shape the points, you just work twice into the first and last stitches on the increase rows, and the 2-row stripes make it easy to count the rows. When you've joined the points, there's no shaping for the rest of the hat; all you need to do is join the back seam, turn up the brim, and pop it on.

ESTIMATED TIME TO COMPLETE

For the first-size hat, 6 hours including tassels.

ABOUT THIS YARN

The wool-mix fingering yarn used for the hat here is a hardwearing mix of 75 percent wool, 25 percent nylon, with 284 yd. (260 m) to a 100-g ball or 142 yd. (130 m) to a 50-g ball.

SIZES

To fit: age 3 to 6 months[**1 to 2**:3 to 4] years

Actual measurement: around head 17(**17¾**:18½) in.

[43(**45**:47) cm]

Figures in parentheses refer to larger sizes. One figure refers to all sizes.

YOU WILL NEED

■ approximately 40(**45**:50) g of wool-mix fingering-weight yarn, in red (A)

■ approximately 30(**35**:40) g of same, in each of blue (B) and yellow (C)

■ D/3 (3.00-mm) crochet hook

GAUGE

19 sts and 24 rows to 4 in. (10 cm) over single crochet using D/3 (3.00-mm) hook. Change hook size if necessary to obtain this gauge.

ABBREVIATIONS

ch = chain; **cont** = continue; **rep** = repeat; **RS** = right side; **sc** = single crochet; **st(s)** = stitch(es); **WS** = wrong side; [ ] = work instructions in brackets as directed.

TIPS

■ For a neat edge pull through the last loop of the last stitch in the new color.

■ Carry the yarn not in use along the edge of the work, twisting yarns when changing colors to keep the edge neat.

■ You could work the hat in just two colors or change color for each stripe. Or if you'd like to make the hat all in one color, you'll need approximately 90(**100**:110) g of wool-mix fingering.

HAT

Using A, join yarn in 15th(**16th**:17th)sc of first point, make 12 ch. Fasten off and join end of ch to 15th(**16th**:17th)sc of 2nd point. Join A in 6th ch from first point.

Row 1 (WS) 1ch, 1sc in same ch as join, 1sc in each of next 5ch, * 1sc in each of next 14(**15**:16)sc of first point, 1sc in seam, 1sc in each of next 14(**15**:16)sc of first point *, 1sc in base of each of next 12ch, rep from * to * around 2nd point, 1sc in each of next 6ch, 1sc in same ch as first sc, turn. 83(**87**:91) sts. Change to B.

Row 2 1ch, [1sc in each sc] to end.

Cont in sc stripe patt, work 46(**50**:54) rows. Fasten off. Darn in ends.

TO FINISH

Press lightly. Darn in all ends. Join back seam in same way as points, reversing seam for turn-up brim. Using A, make 2 tassels approximately 4¼ in. (11 cm) long and sew on points.

HAT POINTS

1st point Using A, make 5(**7**:9)ch.

Row 1 (RS) 1sc in 2nd ch from hook, [1sc in each ch] to end. 4(**6**:8) sts.

Row 2 1ch, 1sc in first sc, [1sc in each sc] to end. Row 2 forms sc. Change to B.

Inc row (RS) 1ch, 2sc in first sc, [1sc in each sc] to last sc, 2sc in last sc. 6(**8**:10) sts.

Cont in sc, work 1 row in B, then work 2-row stripes of C, A, and B, while inc 1sc at each end of next 12 RS rows. 30(**32**:34) sts. Patt 4 more rows, ending with 1 row in A. Fasten off.

2nd point Work as given for first point. Overlapping smooth edge one st in front of edge with color changes, join seams of points.

Striped Bootees

Bootees, bed socks, or slipper socks—whichever you need, here they are. Use up scraps of leftover yarn in colors to match the Jester's Hat on page 126 or choose your own color scheme. The bootees are all in single crochet, so they're easy to make. They're worked from the top down with a simple front extension and a separate sole.

ESTIMATED TIME TO COMPLETE

For each first-size boot, 1¾ hours each; for a pair, 3½ hours.

ABOUT THIS YARN

The wool-mix fingering-weight yarn used for the bootees here is a hardwearing mix of 75 percent wool, 25 percent nylon, with 284 yd. (260 m) to a 100-g ball or 142 yd. (130 m) to a 50-g ball.

SIZES

To fit: age 3 to 6 months(**1 to 2**:3 to 4) years
Actual measurement: along sole 3½(**4¼**:5⅛) in. [9(**11**:13) cm]
Figures in parentheses refer to larger sizes. One figure refers to all sizes.

YOU WILL NEED

■ approximately 20(**30**:40) g of wool-mix fingering-weight yarn, in red (A)
■ approximately 15(**20**:25) g of same in each of blue (B) and yellow (C)
■ D/3 (3.00-mm) crochet hook

GAUGE

19 sts and 24 rows to 4 in. (10 cm) over single crochet worked in rows, using D/3 (3.00-mm) hook. Change hook size if necessary to obtain this gauge.

ABBREVIATIONS

ch = chain; **cont** = continue; **foll** = following; **patt** = pattern; **RS** = right side; **sc** = single crochet; **ss** = slip stitch; **st(s)** = stitch(es); **WS** = wrong side; [ ] = work instructions in brackets as directed.

TIPS

■ Babies' and children's feet vary in size, so make a sole first and compare it with a shoe that fits.
■ When working the sole, take care not to count the slipstitch at the end of each round as a stitch.
■ Like the hat, you can invent your own stripe pattern or make the bootees all in one color.

BOOTEE TOP

Make 27(**35**:39)ch.
Row 1 (RS) 1sc in 2nd ch from hook, 1sc in each ch to end. 26(**34**:38) sts.
Row 2 1ch, [1sc in each sc] to end.
Row 2 forms sc. Cont in stripe patt as given for hat on page 124, work 18(**24**:30) more rows, so ending with a stripe in A. Fasten off.

Shape instep With RS facing, join B to 9th(**12th**:13th)sc.
Row 1 1ch, 1sc in same place as join, 1sc in each of next 9(**11**:13)sc, turn. 10(**12**:14) sts.
Cont in stripe patt, work 10(**12**:14) rows.
Dec row 1ch, skip first sc, 1sc in each of next 8(**10**:12)sc. Fasten off.

Foot With RS facing, join B at beg of last row before instep.
Row 1 1ch, 1sc in each of first 8(**11**:12)sc, 11(**13**:15)sc in row ends up first side of instep, 8(**10**:12)sc across toe, 11(**13**:15)sc in row ends down 2nd side of instep and 1sc in each of last 8(**11**:12)sc. 46(**58**:66) sts.
Work 4 rows, so ending with 1 row in A. Fasten off.

SOLE

Using A, wind yarn around finger to form a ring.
Round 1 (RS) 1ch, 8sc in ring, pull end to close ring, ss in first sc, make 5(**7**:9)ch.
Round 2 1ch, 2sc in 2nd ch from hook, 1sc in each of next 3(**5**:7)ch, 1sc in each of next 2sc, 2sc in each of next 4sc, 1sc in each of foll 2sc, 1sc in base of next 3(**5**:7)ch, 2sc in base of foll ch, ss in first sc. 22(**26**:30) sts.
Round 3 1ch, 1sc in first sc, 1sc in each of next 8(**10**:12)sc, 2sc in next sc, 1sc in each of next 2sc, 2sc in foll sc, 1sc in each of next 8(**10**:12)sc, 2sc in last sc, ss in first sc. 26(**30**:34) sts.
Round 4 1ch, 2sc in each of first 2sc, 1sc in

each of next 8(**10**:12)sc, 2sc in each of foll
2sc, 1sc in each of next 2sc, 2sc in each of
foll 2sc, 1sc in each of next 8(**10**:12)sc, 2sc in
each of last 2sc, ss in first sc. 34(**38**:42) sts.
Round 5 1ch, 1sc in first sc, 2sc in next sc,
1sc in each of foll 12(**14**:16)sc, 2sc in next sc,
1sc in each of foll 4sc, 2sc in next sc, 1sc in
each of foll 12(**14**:16)sc, 2sc in next sc, 1sc in
last sc. 38(**42**:46) sc.
Round 6 1ch, 1sc in first sc, 2sc in next sc,
1sc in each of foll 13(**15**:17)sc, 2sc in next sc,
1sc in each of foll 6sc, 2sc in next sc, 1sc in

each of foll 13(**15**:17)sc, 2sc in next sc, 1sc in
last sc, ss in first sc. 42(**46**:50) sts.
Round 7 1ch, 1sc in first sc, 2sc in next sc,
1sc in each of foll 14(**16**:18)sc, 2sc in next sc,
1sc in each of foll 8sc, 2sc in next sc, 1sc in
each of foll 14(**16**:18)sc, 2sc in next sc, 1sc in
last sc, ss in first sc. 46(**50**:54) sts.
2nd and 3rd sizes Cont in same way as
Round 7, increasing at heel and toe, working
1 more sc at each side and 2 more sc between
toe increases each time.
2nd size Work 2 more rounds.

These striped bootees
keep little feet cozy.

3rd size Work 3 more rounds.
All sizes 46(**58**:66) sts. Darn in all ends.

TO FINISH

Using A and with WS together, join sole to
last row of top of boot with sc. Fasten off.
Join back seam as for Jester's Hat on page
126, reversing seam for turndown tops.

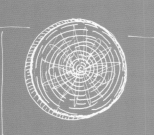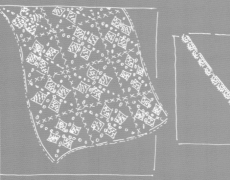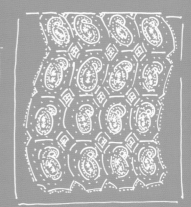

Home

Flowery Paisley Throw

It's fascinating to see the characteristic paisley shape appear as you work these motifs. The stitches are all straightforward; although the joining can be a bit fiddly, the effect is really worth it. The throw in the picture is made from 20 paisley blocks with simple filler squares in between. You can adjust the size of your throw by changing the number of motifs you join together.

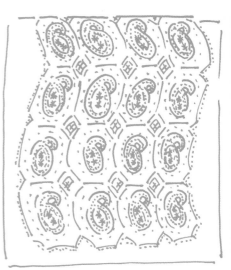

ESTIMATED TIME TO COMPLETE

For each motif, 40 minutes; throw 24 hours.

ABOUT THIS YARN

A variety of wool and wool-mix DK or sport-weight yarns were used to make this throw, with an average of 131 yd. (120 m) to a 50-g ball.

SIZE

Width 37¼ in. (95 cm); **length** 41 in. (104 cm)

YOU WILL NEED

■ 5 x 50-g balls of wool-mix DK in shades of cream
■ 4 x 50-g balls of same or similar DK in shades of lime and grass green
■ E/4 (3.50-mm) crochet hook

GAUGE

Each paisley motif measures 4½ x 7½ in. (11 x 19 cm); each joined block measures 7½ x 10½ in. (19 x 26 cm), all when pressed, using E/4 (3.50-mm) hook. Change hook size if necessary to obtain this size block.

ABBREVIATIONS

ch = chain; **dc** = double crochet; **rep** = repeat; **RS** = right side; **sc** = single crochet; **sp(s)** = space(s); **ss** = slip stitch; **tr** = triple; **WS** = wrong side; **[ ]** = work instructions in brackets as directed.

NOTES

■ The instructions do not give color changes; you can make the motifs in any combination of colors that you prefer.
■ For the effect in the picture, work alternate paisley motifs in shades of lime and grass green sandwiched between cream for the center flowers and outer edging. Use cream for the edging of each motif, and alternate green and cream for the filler squares.
■ Yarn amounts given are approximate. As with any scrap-yarn project, different sport-weight or DK yarns may vary in length-to-weight ratio.

TIPS

■ The paisley motifs and the edging that joins them are given separately to make it easier to carry the work around. If you find it easier, just continue with the edging and join motifs as you work them.
■ The instructions explain how to join the pieces with crochet; this gives a very neat finish, but if you prefer, you could omit the joins from the last round of the block edging and the filler squares, then sew the pieces together.
■ You can use any color scheme you like. Shades of blue or natural work well, or you can use up even the tiniest scraps of leftover yarn by making each paisley and filler square a wild random mix of colors with a dark contrast for the block edging.
■ When changing colors, remember to pull through the last part of the last stitch of a round with the new color.

This unusual throw can go from bedroom to living room.

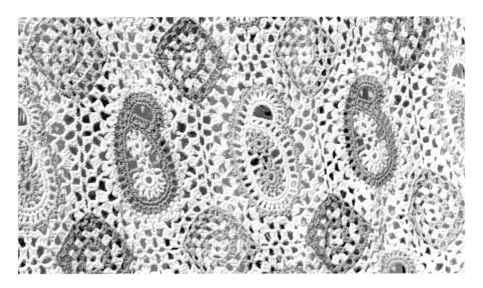

PAISLEY MOTIF

First flower Make 6ch, ss in first ch to form a ring.

Round 1 (RS) 1ch, 8sc in ring, ss in first sc.

Round 2 1ch, 1sc in first sc, 3ch, [1sc in next sc, 3ch] 7 times, ss in first sc. Fasten off.

2nd flower Make 7ch, ss in first ch to form a ring.

Round 1 (RS) 1ch, 10sc in ring, ss in first sc.

Round 2 1ch, 1sc in first sc, 4ch, [1sc in next sc, 4ch] 7 times, 1sc in next sc, 2ch, 1sc in a 3ch sp of first flower, 2ch, 1sc in next sc, 2ch, 1sc in next 3ch sp of first flower, 2ch, ss in first sc. Fasten off.

Border Join yarn in first flower in 3rd sp before join.

Round 1 (RS) 1ch, 1sc in same sp as join, [2ch, 1sc in next sp] twice, 2ch, 1dc in sp with join, 2ch, now work around 2nd flower, 1tr in next sp with join, [2ch, 1sc in next sp] 8 times, 2ch, 1tr in sp with join, 2ch, 1dc in sp with join on first flower, [2ch, 1sc in next sp] 3 times, 2ch, ss in first sc, make 15ch, do not turn.

Round 2 2sc in 2nd ch from hook, [1sc in next ch, 2sc in foll ch] 4 times, 1sc in each of next 4ch, 1sc in same place as ss, [2sc in next sp, 1sc in next st] 17 times, 1sc in last sp, ss in lower loop of each of first 3ch, turn.

Round 3 (WS) 1ch, 1dc in first sc, [1ch, skip 1sc, 1dc in next sc] 11 times, 1ch, 1dc in next sc] 9 times, [1ch, skip 1sc, 1dc in

next sc] 13 times, [1ch, 1dc in next sc] 10 times, 1ch, skip 1sc, 1dc in next sc, place RS together to work 1sc in 5th sp from beginning of this round, ss in next dc, ss in next sp, insert hook in end ch of Round 1 and ss to next st. Fasten off.

With RS facing, join yarn in sp made when joining end ch to 3rd round.

Round 4 1ch, 1sc in same sp as join, [1sc, 3ch, 1sc] in each of next 39 sps, 1sc in last free sp, 1ch, 1sc in first 3ch sp, 1ch, 1sc in same place as sc in last free sp, 1sc in sp made with joined ch, ss in first sc. 40 3ch sps. Fasten off. Make 19 more paisley motifs.

EDGE AND JOIN MOTIFS

1st block With RS facing, join yarn in sp to the left of the two joined sps in the crook of the paisley.

Round 1 1sc in same sp as join, 5ch, [skip 1sp, 5sc in next sp, 5ch] 19 times, 4sc in first sp, ss in first sc.

Round 2 1sc in 5ch sp, 2ch, 2dc in same sp, 3ch, 3dc in same sp, * 3ch, 1sc in next sp, 3ch, [3dc, 3ch, 3dc] in foll sp, rep from * 8 more times, 3ch, 1sc in next sp, 1ch, 1dc in 2nd ch.

Round 3 1sc in dc sp, 2ch, 1dc in dc sp, * 2ch, [2dc, 2ch, 2dc] in next sp, [2ch, 2dc in foll sp] twice, rep from * 3 times, 2ch, 2sc in next sp, 2ch, ** [2dc in next sp, 2ch] twice, [2dc, 2ch, 2dc] in foll sp, 2ch, rep from ** 3 times, [2dc in next sp, 2ch] twice, 2sc in foll

sp, 2ch, 2dc in next sp, 2ch, ss in 2nd ch. Fasten off.

2nd Block Work as first block, joining 3rd round to 8 sps of first long side on the right of first motif by working 1ch, 1sc in adjacent sp, 1ch, between dc groups instead of 2ch. Edge and join 3rd motif to 2nd motif, 4th motif to 3rd motif and 5th motif to 4th motif in the same way. Join 6th motif to top edge of 1st motif, 7th motif to side edge of 6th motif and top edge of 2nd motif, 8th motif to 7th and 3rd motifs, 9th motif to 8th and 4th motifs and 10th motif to 9th and 5th motifs. Edge and join two more lines of 5 paisley motifs in the same way.

FILLER SQUARE

Make 8ch, ss in first ch to form a ring.

Round 1 (RS) 1sc in ring, 5ch, [2dc in ring, 3ch] 3 times, 1dc in ring, ss in 2nd ch.

Round 2 1sc in first 3ch sp, 5ch, 2dc in same 3ch sp, [2ch, 2dc in next 3ch sp, 3ch, 2dc in same 3ch sp] 3 times, 2ch, 1dc in first 3ch sp, ss in 2nd ch.

Round 3 1sc in first 3ch sp, 5ch, 2dc in same 3ch sp, [2ch, 2dc in next 2ch sp, 2ch, 2dc in next 3ch sp, 3ch, 2dc in same 3ch sp] 3 times, 2ch, 2dc in next 2ch sp, 2ch, 1dc in first 3ch sp, ss in 2nd ch.

Join square in space between blocks.

Round 4 1sc in first 3ch sp, 3ch, 1sc in top right corner sp of first block, 1ch, 1sc in corner sp of 2nd block, 1ch, 2dc in first 3ch sp of square, * [1ch, 1sc in next sp of block edge, 1ch, 2dc in next sp of square] 3 times, 1ch, 1sc in corner sp of 2nd block, 1ch, 1dc in corner sp of next block, 1ch, 2dc in same sp of square as last 2dc, rep from * 2 more times, [1ch, 1sc in next sp of block edge, 1ch, 2dc in next sp of square] twice, 1ch, 1sc in next sp of block edge, 1ch, 1dc in first 3ch sp of square, ss in 2nd ch.

Fasten off. Make and join 11 more filler squares.

TO FINISH

Darn in ends. Press.

Cozy Creamy Afghan

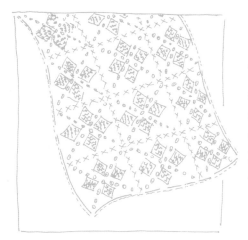

The only stitches you need to know to work this blanket are chain stitch, slip stitch, and double crochet. The squares are a simple variation on a traditional block with bobbles, made by clustering doubles together, adding texture. This is an ideal project to carry around; although the squares are large, there are just six rounds to work, so you can continue your project whenever you have a few spare moments.

ESTIMATED TIME TO COMPLETE

Each square, 25 minutes; 5 hours for 12 blocks, plus 2 hours to join the blocks and edge the blanket. Total time, 7 hours.

ABOUT THIS YARN

Sirdar Spree is a chunky but lightweight 60 percent cotton, 40 percent acrylic yarn, with 149 yd. (136 m) to a 100-g ball.

SIZE

Width 34¼ in. (87 cm); **length** 45¼ in. (115 cm)

YOU WILL NEED

■ 7 x 100-g balls of Sirdar Spree in Limestone, shade 087
■ K/10½ (7.00-mm) and J/10 (6.00-mm) crochet hooks

GAUGE

Each square measures 10 x 10 in. (25 x 25 cm) using K/10½ (7.00-mm) hook. Change hook size if necessary to obtain this size square.

ABBREVIATIONS

ch = chain; **dc** = double crochet; **4dccl** = leaving last loop of each on hook, work 4dc all in same st or sp as directed, yo and pull through 5 loops on hook; **rep** = repeat; **RS** = right side; **sp** = space; **ss** = slip stitch; **st(s)** = stitch(es) **yo** = yarn over hook; [ ] = work instructions in brackets as directed.

NOTES

■ One ball of yarn will make two squares with some left over. If you want to avoid darning in ends while working a square, put this yarn aside until the end and use it to join the squares and edge the blanket.
■ Working into a ring of thread rather than a starting chain gives a neat center. If you weave the starting end between each of the 3ch, you can work over it in the next round and just snip the end off. Otherwise you must darn it in very securely.

TIPS

■ If you darn in ends or work over them as you go, there's no making up to do!
■ Big hooks make for fast work, but they can be clumsy to handle; make sure you turn the hook slightly as you pull loops through so you don't catch or split the yarn.
■ The trick with yarn this thick is to be sure to handle it gently. Make the stitches with a smooth, turning action; don't snatch them through or your gauge could be too tight.
■ If you want to check your gauge before completing the square, each round should be approximately ⅞ in. (2 cm) high.
■ If you want to make a scarf that's 1 square wide by 5 squares long—approximately 12¼ x 56¼ in. (31 x 143 cm)—you'll need 3 x 100-g balls of Spree.
■ If you want a bigger afghan, just work out how many squares you need, allowing 1 in. (3 cm) for each join. Add 1 ball of yarn for every 2 extra squares.

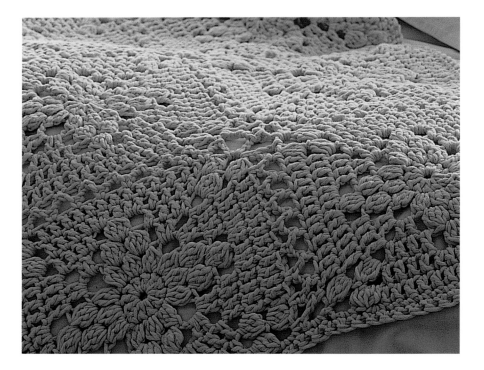

BOBBLE SQUARE

Using K/10½ (7.00-mm) hook, wrap yarn around finger to form a ring.

Round 1 3ch, 11dc in ring, pull end to tighten ring, ss in 3rd ch. 12 sts.

Round 2 3ch, leaving last loop of each st on hook, work 3dc in same place as ss, yo and pull through 4 loops on hook, [1ch, 4dccl in next dc] twice, 5ch, * [4dccl in next dc, 1ch] 3 times, work 4 more ch, rep from *twice, ss in 3rd ch.

Round 3 Ss in first 1ch sp, 3ch, leaving last loop of each st on hook, work 3dc in same place as ss, yo and pull through 4 loops on hook, 1ch, 4dccl in next 1ch sp, * 2ch, [2dc, 2ch] twice in 5ch sp, 4dccl in next 1ch sp, 1ch, 4dccl in next 1ch sp, rep from * twice, 2ch, [2dc, 2ch] twice in 5ch sp, ss in 3rd ch.

Round 4 Ss in first 1ch sp, 3ch, leaving last loop of each st on hook, work 3dc in same place as ss, yo and pull through 4 loops on hook, 2ch, * 1dc in 2ch sp, 1dc in each of next 2dc, [1dc, 2ch, 1dc] in next 2ch sp, 1dc in each of next 2dc, 1dc in foll 2ch sp, 2ch, 4dccl in next 1ch sp, 2ch, rep from * twice, 1dc in next 2ch sp, 1dc in each of next 2dc, [1dc, 2ch, 1dc] in foll 2ch sp, 1dc in each

of next 2dc, 1dc in last 2ch sp, 2ch, ss in 3rd ch.

Round 5 3ch, [2dc in 2ch sp, 1dc in each of next 4dc, 2ch, 4dccl in 2ch sp, 2ch, 1dc in each of next 4dc, 2dc in 2ch sp, 1dc in 4dccl] 4 times, omitting last dc, ss in 3rd ch.

Round 6 3ch, 1dc in each of next 6dc, * 2ch, [4dccl in next 2ch sp, 2ch] twice, 1dc in each of next 13dc, rep from * twice, 2ch, [4dccl in next 2ch sp, 2ch] twice, 1dc in each of next 6dc, ss in 3rd ch.

Fasten off. Darn in ends.

Make 12 bobble squares.

JOIN SQUARES

Using J/10 (6.00-mm) hook, join yarn in corner 2ch sp. With WS together and square with joined yarn in front, join along one edge of two squares by working 2ch, 1sc in corner space of back square, 2ch, 1sc in next 2ch sp of front square, 2ch, 1sc in next 2ch sp of back square, 2ch, miss 1dc, 1sc in next dc of front square, 2ch miss 1dc, 1sc in next dc of back square, continue in this way working into alternate dc, then into spaces at end. Fasten off. Join edges of squares in this way to make the afghan 3 squares by 4 squares.

Filler motifs Work one in each space

between joins at corners of squares. Wind yarn around finger to make a ring.

Round 1 (RS) 1ch, 1sc in ring, 1dc in corner sp of first square, [1sc in ring, 1dc in corner sp of next square] 3 times, pull end to tighten ring, ss in 1st sc. Fasten off. Darn in all ends.

Edging Using K/10½ (7.00-mm) hook and with RS facing, join yarn in a 2ch sp along one edge.

Round 1 Working 2sc in each sp along edge, 1sc in each dc, and 5sc in each corner sp, work one round of sc, ss in first sc, turn.

Round 2 Working 1sc in each sc and 3sc in corner sc, work one round sc, ss in first sc. Fasten off. Darn in all ends.

Chunky yarn, a large hook, and
supersize square motifs mean that
you can make this afghan in a day.

Irish Lace Pillow

Raised flowers and picot mesh make a delicate design, but this pillow is easier than it looks. The front is made from just four motifs joined to make a square, with an extra flower sewn on in the center. And there are no complicated stitches, just the basics: chain, slip stitch, single crochet, half-double and double crochet, combined to create a stunning, decorative effect.

ESTIMATED TIME TO COMPLETE

The pillow front took 7 hours.

ABOUT THIS YARN

Sirdar Pure Cotton 4ply is a smooth 100 percent cotton yarn with a firm twist. It has approximately 370 yd. (338 m) to a 100-g ball.

SIZE

Width 12 in. (30 cm); **length** 12 in. (30 cm)

YOU WILL NEED

- 1 x 100-g balls of Sirdar Pure Cotton 4ply in Stone, shade 025
- C/2 (2.50-mm) crochet hook
- 12 x 12 in. (30 x 30 cm) pillow form with cover

GAUGE

Each 11-round motif measures 5½ x 5½ in. (14 x 14 cm), when pressed, using C/2 (2.50-mm) hook. Change hook size if necessary to obtain this size motif.

ABBREVIATIONS

ch = chain; **dc** = double crochet; **hdc** = half-double crochet; **picot** = 3ch, 1sc in 3rd ch from hook; **rep** = repeat; **RS** = right side; **sc** = single crochet; **sp(s)** = space(s); **ss** = slip stitch; **st(s)** = stitch(es); **[ ]** = work instructions in brackets as directed.

NOTE

It saves a lot of counting back along the chain if you move your finger and thumb up to grip the chain before working the picot, because you can see immediately which chain to work the sc into.

TIPS

- Before pressing, spray the wrong side of the pillow front with starch, press, then turn it over and use the tip of the iron to press each petal of the flowers.
- Make sure that the color you choose for the pillow cover contrasts with the tone of the yarn and shows through behind the crochet.
- If you can't find a pillow with a cover in the color you want, buy plain fabric and make your own cover.

LACY MOTIF

Make 6ch, ss in first ch to form a ring.

Round 1 (RS) 1ch, 12sc in ring, ss in first sc.

Round 2 1ch, 1sc in same place as ss, 4ch, [skip 1sc, 1sc in next sc, 4ch] 5 times, skip 1sc, ss in first sc.

Round 3 [1sc, 1hdc, 3dc, 1hdc, 1sc] in each 4ch sp, ss in first sc.

Round 4 Taking hook behind petals, work 1sc around the stem of first sc of Round 2, 5ch, [1sc around stem of next sc of Round 2, 5ch] 5 times, ss in first sc.

Round 5 [1sc, 1hdc, 5dc, 1hdc, 1sc] in each 5ch sp, ss in first sc.

Round 6 Taking hook behind petals, work 1sc around the stem of first sc of Round 4, 7ch, [1sc around stem of next sc of Round 4, 7ch] 5 times, ss in first sc.

Round 7 [1sc, 1hdc, 7dc, 1hdc, 1sc] in each 7ch sp, ss in first sc.

Round 8 Taking hook behind petals, work 1sc around the stem of first sc of Round 6, 9ch, [1sc around stem of next sc of Round 6, 9ch] 5 times, ss in first sc.

Round 9 [* 1sc, 1ch, 1picot, 2ch, 1picot *, 2ch, 1sc] twice in each of first five 9ch sps and once in last 9ch sp, rep from * to * in last 9ch sp, 1dc in first sc, turn, ss in each of next 2ch, turn.

Round 10 1ch, 1sc between picots in first sp, * 8ch, 1sc between picots in next sp, turn, 1sc in sc, 2ch, 9dc in 8ch sp, 1dc in sc, turn, 1sc in first dc, 3ch, [skip 1dc, 1dc in next dc, 1ch] 4 times, work 2 more ch, ss in next ch and in each of next 2 sts, 1sc in sp between picots, [1ch, 1picot, 2ch, 1picot, 2ch, 1sc between picots in next sp] twice, rep from * 3 more times, omitting last 2ch and 1sc, 1dc in first sc, turn, ss in each of next 2 sts, turn.

Round 11 1sc between picots, * 1ch, 1picot, 2ch, 1picot, 2ch, 1sc in next sp, skipping alternate sps across corner motifs, rep from * to end, omitting last 2ch and 1sc, 1dc in first sc. Fasten off. Darn in ends. Make 3 more lacy motifs.

JOIN MOTIFS

With RS facing, place the first motif at lower right, 2nd motif at top right, 3rd motif at lower left and 4th motif at top left to form a

This pretty pillow is perfect for a bedroom or boudoir and would make a lovely gift.

square with 2 picot loops of each motif to the center. Join yarn in 2nd corner sp on the right edge of first motif. With wrong sides together, hold 2nd motif behind first motif.

Joining row (RS) 1ch, 1sc in same sp as join, * 2ch, 1picot, 2ch, 1sc in corresponding sp of 2nd motif, rep from * working alternately into following sps of first and 2nd motifs until 5 sps of each motif have been joined, 10ch, 1sc in 2nd corner sp at right edge of 3rd motif, join 3rd and 4th motifs in same way as first and 2nd motifs. Fasten off. Join across between motifs in the same way.

Center flower Work as given for first 7 rounds of lacy motif. Fasten off. Darn in all ends.

EDGING

With RS facing, join yarn in first of the two sps at one corner.

Round 1 1ch, 1sc in same sp as join, [5ch, 1sc in next sp] to last sp, 5ch, ss in first sc.

Round 2 1ch, [9sc in corner sp, 5sc in each of next 12 sps] 4 times, ss in first sc.

Round 3 1ch, 1sc in each sc, ss in first sc.

Round 4 3ch, [1picot, skip 1sc, 1dc in next sc] to last sc, 1 picot, skip last sc, ss in 3rd ch. Fasten off. Darn in ends.

TO FINISH

Press according to ball band. Darn in ends. Sew on center flower. Sew pillow front to pillow.

Lace-Edged Tablecloth

This delicate fan edging is created with the simplest of stitches. Although the instructions explain how to edge the tablecloth shown in the picture, the edging is very adaptable. You can work it directly into the fabric or make a separate length and sew it on. You can also change the size of the edging according to the yarn you choose; this tablecloth edging is in a firm fingering-weight cotton yarn. In a finer yarn the edging would make a lovely lingerie trim; in a heavier yarn it would suit a shade or a bedspread.

ESTIMATED TIME TO COMPLETE

For the edging, 7 hours.

ABOUT THIS YARN

The 100 percent cotton yarn used to edge the tablecloth is a firmly twisted fingering with approximately 125 yd. (115 m) to a 50-g ball.

SIZE

Width 38 in. (96.5 cm); **length** 38 in. (96.5 cm)

YOU WILL NEED

- approximately 80 g of fingering-weight cotton yarn in ecru
- B/1 (2.00-mm) crochet hook
- 36½ x 36½ in. (93 x 93 cm) even-weave linen fabric in cream

GAUGE

Edging is 1 in. (2.5 cm) deep; 2 repeats measure 2½ in. (6 cm) using B/1 (2.00-mm) hook. Change hook size if necessary to obtain this gauge.

ABBREVIATIONS

ch = chain; **dc** = double crochet; **foll** = following; **rep** = repeat; **sc** = single crochet; **sp** = space; **ss** = slip stitch; **st(s)** = stitch(es); **[ ]** = work instructions in brackets as directed.

TABLECLOTH

Preparation Pull threads along each edge of the linen to make sure that the fabric is square. Trim if necessary. Pull out 4 threads 18 threads in from each edge. Fold fabric twice along each edge to make a narrow hem that lines up with space left by drawing the threads. Press the hems.

EDGING

Join yarn in approximately 5 threads from a corner space.

Round 1 Inserting hook in gap left by drawing threads to work over hem, work [235sc evenly along edge and 3sc in corner] 4 times, ss in first sc.

Round 2 1ch, 1sc in same place as ss, * [2ch, skip 1sc, 1sc in next sc, skip 2sc, 5dc

TIPS

- Make a test piece to be sure that your edging lies flat when made in the fabric and yarn you've chosen.
- To work the sc row evenly along each edge, place markers to divide each edge into 4. Work 58sc to first marker, 1sc in marker place, remove marker, repeat along edge to corner, work 3sc in corner, then continue in the same way around the tablecloth.
- You can make the edging fit around a smaller or larger cloth; just allow about 1¼ in. (3 cm) more or less fabric for each repeat of the edging and make sure that you work a multiple of 8 plus 3 along each edge and 3 from each corner on Round 1.
- To work a straight edging in a ring, without corners, make a number of chain divisible by 8 and ss in first ch. Make the chain loosely, or your edging may not stretch to fit. Work Round 1 into the chain; on following rounds repeat instructions in brackets to omit corners.
- Check out lace maker's supplies if you prefer to edge your linen tablecloth with linen thread.
- If you're trimming a cotton cloth, work the edging separately and sew it on, because it's not always easy to draw threads in very tightly woven cotton fabric.

Add a personal touch to table linen, bed linen, or clothing with this easy-to-work edging.

in next sc, skip 2sc, 1sc in next sc] 29 times, 2ch, skip 1sc, 1sc in next sc, skip 1sc, 5dc in corner sc, skip 1sc, 1sc in next sc, rep from * 3 more times, omitting last sc and ending ss in first sc.

Round 3 Ss in first sp, 1ch, 1sc in first sp, * 1ch, [1dc in next dc, 1ch] 5 times, 1sc in next sp, rep from * to end, omitting last sc, ending ss in first sc.

Round 4 Ss in each of first ch and dc, 5ch, [1dc in next dc, 2ch] 3 times, 1dc in foll dc, * [1dc in next dc, 2ch] 4 times, 1dc in foll dc, rep from * to end, ss in 3rd ch. Fasten off. Darn in ends.

TO FINISH
Spray with starch and press.

Comfy Round Pillow

A simple progression of increases makes this circular pillow lie flat. The stitch pattern is just alternate rounds of double and single crochet; for the ridged side just work around the stem instead of into the stitches of the previous round.

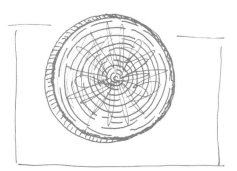

ESTIMATED TIME TO COMPLETE
The pillow took 5 hours.

ABOUT THIS YARN
Debbie Bliss Cotton DK is a matte, smooth 100 percent cotton yarn with 92 yd. (84 m) to a 50-g ball.

SIZE
Circumference 15 in. (38 cm); **depth** 2 in. (5 cm)

YOU WILL NEED
■ 6 x 50-g balls of Debbie Bliss Cotton DK in taupe, shade 019
■ F/5 (4.00-mm) crochet hook
■ round pillow form 15 in. (38 cm) diameter x 2 in. (5 cm) deep

GAUGE
18 rounds in patt measure 15 in. (38 cm); 8 rounds sc measure 2 in. (5 cm) using F/5 (4.00-mm) hook. Change hook size if necessary to obtain this gauge.

ABBREVIATIONS
cont = continue; **ch** = chain; **dc** = double crochet; **foll** = following; **sc** = single crochet; **ss** = slip st; **st(s)** = stitch(es); [ ] = work instructions in brackets as directed.

TIPS
■ Rotate the hook to show the nubbly side of the turning chain; this will help blend it in with the double stitches.
■ To help hide the joins in the rounds, instead of working the ss in the usual way, remove the hook and insert it from the back into the 3rd ch or sc, then catch the loop and pull it through. This is particularly good for joining the sc-around-the-post rounds.

in each of next 6sc, [2dc in foll sc, 1dc in each of next 6sc] to end, ss in 3rd ch. 192 sts.
Round 18 As Round 2.
Cont in sc worked in the usual way for 8 more rounds. Fasten off.
Smooth side Work as given for ridged side but working sc rounds in sts in the usual way until 18 rounds have been completed.

TO FINISH

Darn in ends. Press according to ball band. Inserting pillow form, taking 1 st from each side together each time, join the two sides of the pillow with a round of sc.

This sophisticated but simple pillow gives you a choice of textures.

PILLOW

Ridged side Wind yarn around finger to form a ring.
Round 1 3ch, 11dc in ring, pull end to tighten ring, ss in 3rd ch. 12 sts.
Round 2 and every alt round 1ch, 1sc around the stem of each st, ss in first sc.
Round 3 3ch, 1dc in same place as ss, [2dc in each sc] to end, ss in 3rd ch. 24 sts.
Round 5 As Round 3. 48 sts.
Round 7 3ch, 1dc in same place as ss, 1dc in next sc, [2dc in foll sc, 1dc in next sc] to end, ss in 3rd ch. 72 sts.

Round 9 3ch, 1dc in same place as ss, 1dc in each of next 2sc, [2dc in foll sc, 1dc in each of next 2sc] to end, ss in 3rd ch. 96 sts.
Round 11 3ch, 1dc in same place as ss, 1dc in each of next 3sc, [2dc in foll sc, 1dc in each of next 3sc] to end, ss in 3rd ch. 120 sts.
Round 13 3ch, 1dc in same place as ss, 1dc in each of next 4sc, [2dc in foll sc, 1dc in each of next 4sc] to end, ss in 3rd ch. 144 sts.
Round 15 3ch, 1dc in same place as ss, 1dc in each of next 5sc, [2dc in foll sc, 1dc in each of next 5sc] to end, ss in 3rd ch. 168 sts.
Round 17 3ch, 1dc in same place as ss, 1dc

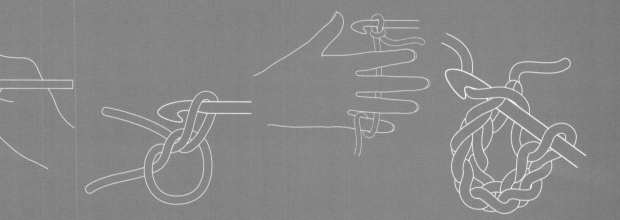

Techniques

Equipment

All crochet stitches are based on the simple action of making loops in a thread with a hook, but although the action is simple, the effects achieved can vary enormously, from a delicate lacy look to a densely textured fabric. If you've never tried crochet before, use a smooth medium-weight-light-colored yarn and a medium-sized hook to try out the basic stitches before starting a project.

YARNS

Wool, cotton, luxury fibers, and man-made fiber mixes in a variety of weights can all be used for crochet. Although smooth, firmly twisted yarns are the classic choice—because the stitches can be seen clearly—interesting effects can be created with the simplest of stitches in textured yarns.

Each project gives details of either the specific or generic yarn type that was used to create the original item. Wherever possible, stick with the recommended yarn, because this will give you the effect shown in the picture. If you have to find a substitute yarn, use the information about fiber content and yardage given with each set of instructions to match the original yarn as closely as possible. If you want to try out one of the designs in an entirely different yarn, the best thing to do is to crochet a sample with just one ball to make sure you're happy with the result before buying a quantity of yarn. As for the amount to buy, you should be aware that this may be quite different, depending on the fiber type and yarn construction. For example, even though both yarns are described as a DK, a design worked in cotton will need more yarn than the same item worked in 100 percent acrylic because cotton is a heavier fiber.

HOOKS

Depending on the size, crochet hooks can be made from steel, aluminum, bamboo, plastic, or wood. Whichever you choose, it's essential that the point and notch at the hook end be smooth. If you are going to use the hook for a lengthy project, choose a handle or a flattened grip instead of a completely round shaft for comfort.

The instructions for each project give a recommended hook size. This is the size that was used to create the original item. However, you may need to use a different hook size to obtain the correct gauge, so it's always a good idea to buy larger and smaller hooks as well as the stated size.

Crochet hooks from left to right: steel with an aluminum handle, bamboo, coated aluminum with a resin handle, aluminum, a larger-sized aluminum-and-resin hook, a larger aluminum hook, and two different types of plastic hook.

ADDITIONAL EQUIPMENT

Other items you'll need in order to make the projects in this book are a tape measure to check your gauge, a blunt-pointed sewing needle or tapestry needle to darn in ends, scissors for snipping yarn, markers to keep track of shaping rows, and blunt-pointed or long quilting pins to hold pieces in place while joining seams.

FOLLOWING THE INSTRUCTIONS

MEASUREMENTS

Each set of instructions provides the item's size in inches, using the yarn and hook size stated at the gauge given. Measurements in centimeters are also given in brackets. The designs were created in metric measurements, so the imperial measurements given are the closest equivalent. For garments, where appropriate, larger sizes are given in parentheses with colons between the figures. The "to fit" sizes are given as a guide for which size to make, but check that you will be happy with the finished actual measurements, because the amount of movement room varies according to the design. If in doubt, compare the actual measurements with a garment you already have at home.

YOU WILL NEED

The yarn amounts given are based on the quantity of yarn used to make the original item. Although the hook size given is that used for the project, it is intended as a guide only. Always change the hook size and try again if you do not achieve the gauge given.

GAUGE

Gauge in crochet can vary enormously, probably because the stitch size is governed not just by the size of the hook but also by the way your fingers tension the yarn. Some of the projects in this book are so simple that you may feel that you can just dive in. But if your gauge is not correct, your time and the cost of the yarn could be wasted.

The best way to check your gauge is to work a sample. Because edge stitches can curl or distort, start with a few more stitches than the amount given as measuring 4 in. (10 cm) and work more rows than given. Count and mark the number of stitches and rows needed in the center of your swatch. Measure between markers. If you get more than 4 in. (10 cm), your crochet is too loose; try again using a smaller hook. If you get less than 4 in. (10 cm), your work is too tight. Try again using a larger hook.

BRACKETS

Instructions in brackets should be repeated as indicated. Brackets are also used to clarify working a group of stitches. One or more asterisks are used to indicate a repeat or a part of the instructions to work again.

Basic Stitches

Crochet is a two-handed craft, with the left hand tensioning the yarn and holding the work while the right hand uses the hook. Because the left hand does much of the work, most left-handed people find that they are comfortable working this way, but left-handers could also reverse the actions, reading left for right and right for left, using a mirror if necessary to check the illustrations. The following instructions explain the way that I like to work. Use other methods if they are more familiar, but do make sure that your stitches are formed correctly.

HOLDING THE HOOK

This is the most flexible way to hold the hook.

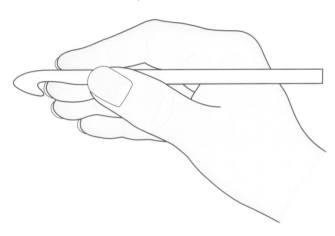

Hold the hook like a pencil with the shaft above your hand; your grip should be light so you can easily extend the hook in a forward-and-back motion.

MAKING A SLIP KNOT

A slip knot is needed to start many projects. It is not counted as a stitch.

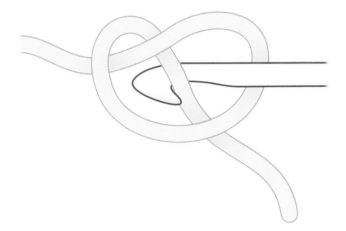

1 Make a loop in the yarn, insert the hook, and catch the back strand of the yarn.

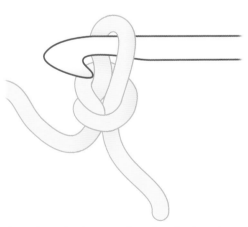

2 Pull a loop through, then gently pull on both ends to tighten the knot and close the loop on the hook.

HOLDING THE YARN

Tensioning the yarn is a very personal thing. I prefer to hold the work with my thumb and first finger; others grip the work between the middle finger and thumb, using the first finger to tension the yarn. However you hold it, as you make stitches, allow the yarn to ease through the fingers, and move the work to keep a grip near the place that a new stitch will be made. If working with fine or slippery yarn, wrap the yarn more times around the middle finger.

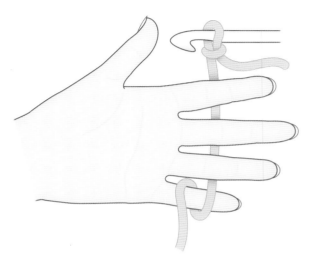

1 Catch the yarn around the little finger of the left hand.

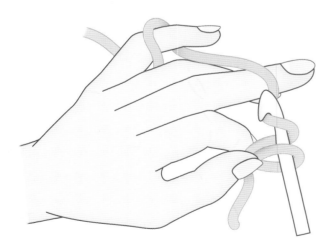

2 Bring the hook toward you to take the yarn over the fingers and hold the tail end of yarn from the slip knot between first finger and thumb. Extend the middle finger to make a space for the hook to catch the yarn.

CHAIN STITCH

Chain stitch may be used as a foundation for other stitches to make spaces or to reach the height of the other stitches when working in rounds or rows.

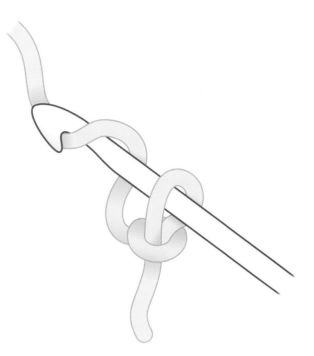

1 With the hook in front of the yarn, dip the tip of the hook to take the yarn over the hook from the back to the front and catch the yarn. This is called yarn over and is the basic movement for all crochet stitches.

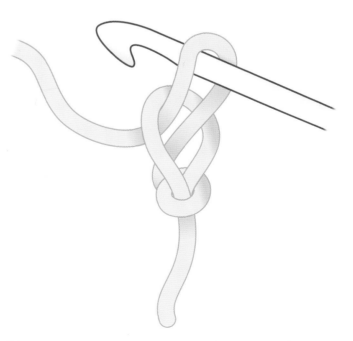

2 Draw a new loop through the loop on the hook to make a new chain loop.

SLIP STITCH

Slip stitch is the shortest stitch; it's used for joining stitches, to work to a new place in the stitch pattern, or to make a decorative surface crochet chain.

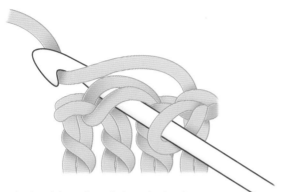

Insert the hook into the stitch and take the yarn over the hook. Draw a new loop through both the stitch and the loop on the hook, ending with one loop on the hook.

SINGLE CROCHET

Single crochet is made in the same way as a slip stitch but with an extra step, giving a stitch that is almost square.

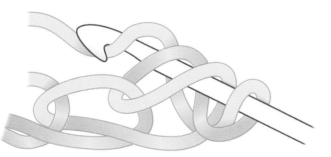

1 Insert the hook into the chain or stitch indicated in the instructions. Yarn over hook, and draw the yarn through the stitch to make two loops on the hook.

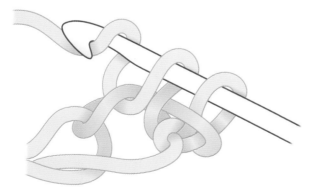

2 Yarn over hook and draw through two loops on the hook, ending with one loop on the hook.

HALF-DOUBLE

This stitch is made in the same way as single crochet, but the yarn is wrapped over the hook.

1 Yarn over hook and insert the hook into the chain or stitch indicated in the instructions.

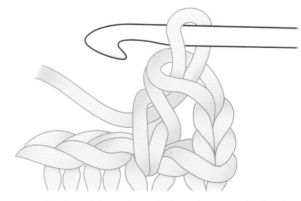

2 Yarn over hook and pull through the stitch to make three loops on the hook.

3 Yarn over hook and draw through three loops on the hook, ending with one loop on the hook.

WORKING LONGER STITCHES

Triple, double triple, and so on are all worked in the same way as a double, but with one more wrapping of the yarn over the hook for each longer stitch, giving one more step when drawing through two loops at a time.

Here's the number of times to wrap the yarn over the hook when making these longer stitches.

Type of Stitch	Number of Times to Wrap
Triple	twice
Double triple	three
Triple triple	four
Quadruple triple	five

FASTENING OFF

The first method is the most usual way of fastening off and is the most secure. The second method makes a neat finish, especially when working motifs.

DOUBLE CROCHET

Working the wrapped yarn makes a longer stitch. Work steps 1 and 2 as given for half-double.

1 Yarn over hook and pull through the first two loops on the hook. Making two loops on the hook, take the yarn over the hook again.

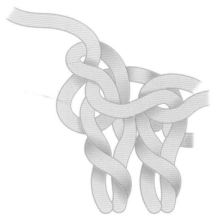

FIRST METHOD

After the last stitch pull another loop through, cut the yarn, and pull the end through.

2 Pull the yarn through the two loops, ending with one loop on the hook.

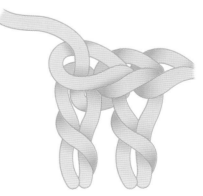

SECOND METHOD

After the last stitch cut the yarn and pull the end through. Darn in the end very securely.

VARIATIONS ON THE STITCHES

All the standard stitches are worked under two strands of the starting chain or under both strands at the top of a stitch—but there are variations in placing the hook and making the stitches, which give different effects.

INSERT HOOK INTO ONE STRAND ONLY

This can be used practically, when working into both sides of a starting chain, or decoratively to open up a fabric. Simply take the hook under one strand, either at the front or at the back of the stitch.

INSERT HOOK BETWEEN STITCHES

This can be practical if the fabric is too fine or too firm to insert the hook in the usual way, or it can open up the fabric and make it quicker to work. The hook is placed, as directed, between the stitches of the previous row.

INSERT HOOK IN THE SIDE OF A STITCH

This is used when making a single or a double crochet chain. For a single crochet chain make a slip knot and two chains. Insert the hook in the first chain and work a single crochet stitch. For each following stitch, insert the hook under the threads at the side of the previous stitch. For a double crochet chain make a slip knot and three chains. Take the yarn over the hook, then insert the hook in the third chain and complete the double crochet in the usual way. For each following

stitch, insert the hook under two strands at the base of the previous stitch. Single and double chains make a more flexible edge than an ordinary starting chain; they are also easier to count.

SURFACE CHAIN

This decorative effect is made by working a slip stitch through the fabric. Hold the yarn under the fabric. Insert the hook in the fabric and pull a loop through. Move the hook along, insert in the fabric, and pull the yarn through the fabric and the loop on the hook to make a new loop on the hook.

WORKING AROUND THE STEM

Any type of crochet stitch can be worked around rather than into the top loops of a stitch. Taking the hook to the front will make the stitch lie on the surface of the work, giving a textured effect. Taking the hook behind will cause the fabric of the previous row to lift forward, as when working the petals of a flower. For a single crochet around the stem, take the hook behind and insert it from right to left around the stem of the designated stitch in the previous row, yarn over hook and pull through to make two loops on the hook, yarn over hook and pull through to make one loop on the hook.

CRAB STITCH

This is simply single crochet worked backward to give a twisted edge. Crab stitch spreads the edge slightly, so there's no need to increase to turn a corner. If a straight edge flutes, either skip the occasional stitch or use a smaller hook.

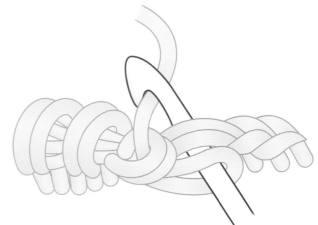

Do not turn the work at the end of the last row. Insert the hook in the last stitch to the right, yarn over hook, and pull through to make two loops twisted on the hook. Yarn over hook again and pull through making one loop on the hook. Repeat in the stitches along the edge or in row ends if necessary.

GROUPING STITCHES

Stitches of any length can be grouped or worked together to increase or decrease the number of stitches in a row or for a decorative effect.

INCREASE, FAN, OR SHELL

Working two or more complete stitches into the same stitch can be a method of increasing to shape a fabric, part of a decorative stitch pattern, or an edging. Any stitch can be used, and the amount of stitches worked varies. In this example three double crochet stitches are worked into one double in the row below.

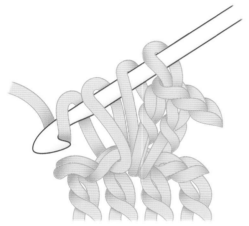

Inserting the hook in the same stitch each time, work three double crochet stitches. The stitches are held together at the bottom but not at the top, making a fan shape.

DECREASE OR CLUSTER

Working two or more partial stitches and taking them together at the top to make one stitch gives a decrease when working a fabric or a cluster in a stitch pattern. The example shows decreasing by taking three doubles together.

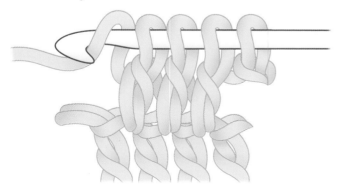

Leaving the last loop of each stitch on the hook, work a double into each of the next three stitches, making four loops on the hook. Yarn over hook and pull through all four loops to join the stitches together at the top and make one loop on the hook.

BOBBLE

When a cluster is worked into one stitch, a bobble is made. The example shows three double crochet stitches worked together, but if the stitches used for the bobble are longer than the background stitches, the bobble will stand away from the surface.

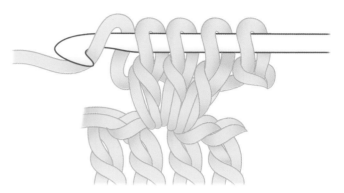

Yarn over hook and insert the hook in the stitch, yarn over hook and pull through. Do not complete the stitch; leave the last loop on the hook and work two more partial double crochet stitches, each time leaving one more loop on the hook, making four loops on the hook. Yarn over hook and pull through all four loops.

POPCORN

This kind of bobble is made from complete stitches. The example shows five double crochet stitches worked in a chain space and taken together, but a popcorn can be placed in any stitch and be made up of any practical number or combination of stitches.

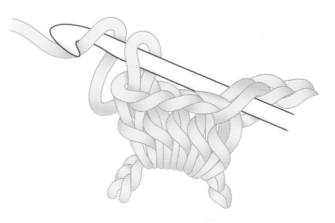

Inserting the hook in the same place each time, work five complete doubles. Slip the hook out of the last loop. Insert the hook into the top of the first stitch, then into the last loop, yarn over hook, and pull through.

Creating a Fabric

Although there are an infinite number of variations, basically there are two ways of making a crochet fabric. Either the stitches can be made on a starting chain and the work turned at the end of each row, or a series of motifs can be worked in the round and joined together.

WORKING IN ROWS

When making a starting chain, don't count the loop on the hook. The chain should be made quite loosely—tight chain will be difficult to work into, and the edge will pull in. For an even, loose chain use a hook one or two sizes larger. When working into the base chain, take the hook under two strands of each chain loop unless instructed otherwise. Each row of the instructions will tell you where to place the hook and which stitch to work. Simply turn the work at the end of each row so the right and the wrong sides face alternately. The instructions will tell you how many turning chain to work or how to cope with the edge stitches. Wherever possible, join in new yarn at the start of a row.

SINGLE CROCHET IN ROWS

A single chain is worked at the start of each row to bring the yarn up to the height needed to work in single crochet. This chain is not worked into on the following row, and it is not counted as a stitch.

DOUBLE CROCHET IN ROWS

Double crochet rows often start with three chain to bring the yarn up to the height needed. This counts as a stitch, and the first stitch of the previous row is skipped to compensate. This can leave a gap between the edge and the next stitch. Depending on the design, the first chain is frequently replaced with a single crochet worked directly into the first stitch, then two chains are worked to bring the yarn up to the height needed to work a row of double crochet.

WORKING MOTIFS

Motifs are worked from the center outward. The starting point can be a ring of chains or a ring made with a loop of yarn. When working in rounds without turning, the right side is always facing. To create some motifs or to match stitch patterns worked in rows, motifs can be turned during or at the end of a round. The instructions will tell you how to join at the end of each round and how many chain to work to match the height of the stitches in the next round.

WORKING INTO A RING OF YARN

Rings of yarn can be drawn up tightly to make a neat, unobtrusive center. Always darn in the yarn end securely.

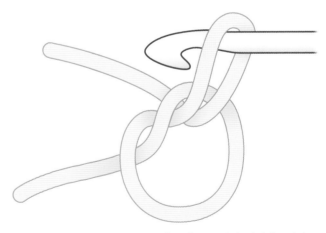

Wind the yarn once around the first finger of the left hand. Insert the hook in the ring, yarn over hook and pull through ring, yarn over hook and pull through to make the first chain. Work stitches into the ring, then pull the end to tighten the ring before joining the round.

JOINING CHAIN STITCHES IN A ROUND

Chains give a very firm start. Three or four chains will give a small hole at the center; more chains will give a larger hole.

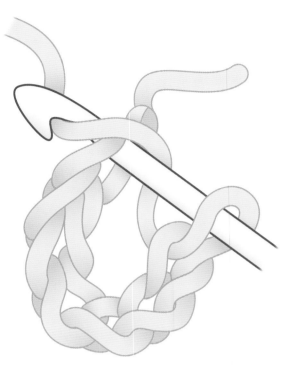

1 Make the starting chain, as indicated in the instructions, insert the hook in the first chain, and take the yarn over the hook.

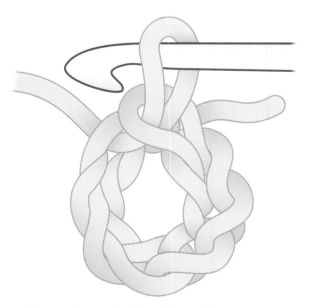

2 Pull the yarn through the first chain and the loop on the hook.

FINISHING

The instructions provide the working order when making up the projects. Some of the designs are worked in the round, so there is a minimum of making up. Garments worked in flat pieces can be sewn together or joined with crochet. Placing markers and pinning seams together will help to match the rows and give a neater finish.

PRESSING OR BLOCKING

Always check the ball band for how the yarn should be washed and pressed. If in doubt, test a sample before making up the garment. To block the pieces, pin them out to size. Always use a padded ironing board so the stitches are not crushed. Items in man-made fibers should never be pressed. Spray them lightly with water and leave to dry under several folded towels. Most natural-fiber yarns can be lightly steam pressed. Work on the wrong side, lifting the iron as you move it across the work, because pushing the iron could stretch the fabric.

SEWING SEAMS

The best way to join the pieces is with right sides facing. Working in mattress stitch, take the yarn under one stitch from each side alternately to match the rows. Take in either whole stitches or two threads of each stitch from each side to reduce the bulk. Otherwise, place the right sides together and oversew the seams.

CROCHET SEAMS

Joining a seam with crochet gives a firm, neat chain edge. Crochet seams are normally worked from the wrong side—the instructions will tell you if they are intended to be decorative and should be worked with the right side facing you. Just insert the hook under one edge stitch from each side together each time, and work in single crochet.

CARE OF CROCHET ITEMS

Store crochet garments folded flat. If you put them on a hanger, they will droop. Follow the recommended wash code for the yarn as given on the ball band. If in doubt, hand wash and dry flat, at least for the first time, so you can monitor the result. If using a washing machine, treat any stains, then turn the garment inside out before washing and reshape it while it is still damp.

Yarn Suppliers

IN THE UNITED STATES

Debbie Bliss, Noro, and Sirdar
Knitting Fever, Inc.
315 Bayview Avenue
Amityville, NY 11701
tel: 516 546 3600
website: www.knittingfever.com

Elle
Unicorn Books and Crafts, Inc.
1138 Ross Street
Petaluma, CA 94954
tel: 707 762 3362
e-mail: dcodling@unicornbooks.com

Rowan
Rowan USA
4 Townsend West
Suite 8
Nashua, NH 03064
tel: 603 886 5041/5043
e-mail: wfibers@aol.com

IN CANADA

Debbie Bliss, Noro, Rowan, and Sirdar
Diamond Yarn
155 Martin Ross Avenue, Unit 3
Toronto, ON M3J 2L9
tel: 416 736 6111
website: www.diamondyarn.com

IN AUSTRALIA

Debbie Bliss and Noro
Prestige Yarns (PTY) Ltd.
P. O. Box 39
Bulli, NSW 2516
tel: 02 4285 6669
website: www.prestigeyarns.com

Rowan
Cottonfields Crafts and Yarns
263 Stirling Highway
Claremont, WA 6010
tel: 08 9383 4410
website: www.cottonfields.net.au

Sunspun
185 Canterbury Road
Canterbury, VIC 3126
tel: 03 9830 1609
website: www.sunspun.com.au

IN NEW ZEALAND

Rowan
Knit World
PO Box 30 645
Lower Hutt
tel: 04 586 4530
website: www.knitting.co.nz

IN SOUTH AFRICA

Elle
Saprotex International (PTY) Ltd.
P O Box 1293
East London
5200 South Africa
tel: 043 798 4200
website: www.knit1now.net

IN THE UNITED KINGDOM

Debbie Bliss and Noro
Designer Yarns
Units 8–10
Newbridge Industrial Estate
Pitt Street
Keighley, West Yorkshire BD21 4PQ
tel: 01535 664222
website: www.designeryarns.uk.com

Elle
Quadra UK Ltd.
Tey Grove
Elm Lane
Feering
Essex CO5 9ES
tel: 01376 573802
e-mail: quadrauk@aol.com
website: www.knit1now.co.uk

Rowan
Rowan Yarns
Green Lane Mill
Holmfirth
West Yorkshire HD9 2DX
tel: 01484 681881
website: www.knitrowan.com

Sirdar
Sirdir Spinning Ltd.
Flanshaw Lane
Alverthorpe
Wakefield
West Yorkshire WF2 9ND
tel: 01924 371501
website: www.sirdar.co.uk

Index

Author's Acknowledgments

I would like to thank everyone who helped me with this book,
especially Cindy Richards for giving me the opportunity to work on this project
and for her support, taste, and enthusiasm. Thanks also to Liz Dean for her calm
guidance and editing, without you Liz, I may never have finished!

Thanks to Debbie Bliss and all at Designer Yarns, Mike Cole and all at Elle,
Kate Buller and all at Rowan and David Rawson, Caroline Powell, and
all at Sirdar for the inspirational yarns.

For help with turning ideas into reality, thank you to Betty Speller
for the Textured Cardigan Coat and to Lesley Stanfield for the Lacy Victorian
Shawl. Many thanks to Tino Tedaldi for the lovely photographs, Sue Rowlands
for the styling, and especially to Sally Powell for her care in bringing the visuals
together. Thanks to Roger Hammond for designing the book. Thanks to the
models: Francoise Wolff, Simona Busimuco, Eleanor Reilly, Amit Dhaliwal,
Louise MacSweeney, Daisy MacSweeney, and Silvia Arganda and baby.

Finally a huge thank you to Sue Horan for her excellent, patient, and through
checking of my instructions.

I would like to dedicate this book to my mother,
HILDA GRIFFITHS
in memory of her life July 19, 1917 to November 6, 2006.